Fitness & Health for the Busy Professional

I0450358

Fitness & Health for the Busy Professional:

Tips from Professionals for Professionals

**By Master Trainer Troy Bonar
"The Samurai of Success"™**

Dedication:

To all those busy people making things happen, it is your moment to take time for yourself and have the fitness level you really deserve.

Foreword
By Master Troy A. Bonar

I am just like most of you, as a matter of fact, I am working on this book while I am waiting for a flight.

I used to teach martial arts full time, I was working out 6 days a week and 6 hours a day.

I could eat what I wanted because I was burning calories constantly.

I stopped teaching full time and had a life change, an injury slowed me down significantly, I had to use medical steroids to help repair the damage and could not use my right side fully for over 6 months; I was no longer able to work out like I had. Within a year I had gained 40 pounds, and the following year, another 50. I maxed my weight at around 300 pounds. I had been a fighting fit 200 before the incident.

I took a full time position in which I travel 90% of the time, so I understand how it works, driving, riding, flying, eating out all the time, big dinners with clients, drinks. I was there just like you.

One day I was teaching a seminar and one side of the room was covered in floor to ceiling mirrors. This was April 15 and 16. I remember because it was tax time. I saw myself for 2 days during my workshop. I decided I had enough, I was losing respect for myself and I can imagine what other people were thinking. Unfortunately people do judge your appearance when it comes to business and your personal interactions.

I went back to my books, I had taught martial arts, I was a Certified Personal Trainer, I have studied homeopathic medicine, Nutrition, etc; but I knew I had to do something

I had never done before to fit the new schedule of my current occupation.

I had to make those small changes in my life, I had to make the decision and I had to take action.

You have already started on the right track by taking action to invest in this book.

Keep on investing in yourself, and you will have a huge success.

Keep it moving and reduce your intake.

I believe that you can be fit and be professional. I look forward to hearing about your success.

This book is full of great tips from other busy people and health and fitness professionals who are dealing with the same issues you face each day.

Also included is a resource section which has wonderful products and services specially designed for busy people like us.

I have mixed in letters from professionals with the meat of this book, and I think you will find that those letters have so much better content than what was written on the page.

Enjoy this book that was written in a quick read format.... Because I know you are busy... Thank yourself for investing some extra time into your health and fitness!

Here's to your health and your future success!-

"Live, Love, Laugh, and Be Happy."

Troy A. Bonar MST

INTRODUCTION

Fit exercise into your busy schedule? That's as absurd as saying that there are eight days in a week!

First off, Maybe you've never exercised before or engaged regularly in a sport; secondly, you've never been into the fitness crowd and have had meager time for such pursuits, and third, you're far too busy to even think of exercise.

In other words, **YOU'RE JUST NOT INTO IT**.

Of course your friends talk about it and rave about the latest fitness craze, but you've seen it too often: some of them are on the "on-again-off-again" treadmill / stair master mania, and you wonder why they haven't shred the fat that they're desperately still trying to hide.

Seeing what your friends go through and not seeing any results, you cling to the notion that your total lack of interest is justified.

You're not the least bit inclined to engage in these circus-like contortions or do those mindless freestyle strokes in the water. That would only encroach into your already busy schedule of juggling family, home and career. These three combined – Significant Other/children/work are your exercise.

Yup, we've got a problem.

That mindset is like a seething volcano that's about to erupt. If you stubbornly cling to the notion that the "fat to trim" concept is merely a myth and a figment of the imagination of a handful of oddballs, your health could be going into "eruption mode" soon, like a restless volcano.

Have you looked at your body lately? Have you taken stock of your overall physical well-being?

Before tackling the idea of fitting exercise into your busy schedule, it might be better if we start with the concepts of self-assessment and then familiarize ourselves with the disease-prevention aspect of exercise.

Once you've accepted the fact that your body needs overhauling, and that exercise is good for your health – then we can talk about some of the ways that you can include exercise into your roller-coaster existence.

This book in your hands right now (or on your screen!) is your KEY to fitting exercise into your life. And rest assured, this book already assumes that you're a busy person with a life to lead; and that's why the tips in here are **specifically designed to fit in with your busy lifestyle!**

To keep things organized and simple, this book is broken down into five easy sections:

Section 1: Assessing Physical Damage

And Accepting the Importance of Exercise

Section 2: No Matter How Busy you Are, there are Ways you can Exercise

Section 3: Busy Traveler? You can Fit Exercise into your Trips

Section 4: Exercise Aids To Go

Section 5: Information / Resources for the Hurried and Harried

Read them in order, or if you wish, focus on the section that is most relevant to you right now. Regardless of how you choose to read this book, you can be confident of one thing: once you apply the advice within these pages, your busy life will include something new and important: exercise!

1

Section 1: Assessing Physical Damage and Accepting the Importance of Exercise

Do you think of your body the way you think of your car? When a few lucky individuals acquire a sports car that boasts of the best automotive engineering available today, watch them read the maintenance manuals religiously.

They take their car for inspection even if it purrs like a kitten and take it for repairs as soon as something does not feel right. And they're very concerned. The longevity and reliability of their vehicle is very important. They don't want to be broken down along the road, or have to fix something costly because they didn't perform the proper maintenance.

People who keep up with their vehicles are planning ahead and are going to have a safer experience. You can also find great Automobile tips in my book, Driving Safety: The Road Warriors Guide to Highway Survival.

That car is their most prized possession, a symbol of all the long and hard hours they put on the job so they could finally acquire it. Or it is their primary source of transportation. It cost an arm and a leg, so taking care of it is logically, their # 1 priority.

But how important is the *person* that drives that car? Shouldn't that person – shouldn't **you** – be the #1 priority?

Lifespan and Physical Appearance

The average life span of men and women is 80 years, give or take a few years. The painful truth is, a <u>significant</u> number of men and women look and feel 80 before they even make it to the first half of their life! You spot the tell-tale signs from their physical appearance:

- ✗ sagging dry skin
- ✗ unsightly posture

- ✗ uneven and unsteady walk (they need to drag around those heavy pounds)
- ✗ aching joints
- ✗ sporting the "I'm not happy because I look terrible" look

Now, if their appearance is *this* bad, imagine what the inside machinery is like! Most likely, it's even worse:

- ✗ clogged vessels
- ✗ inefficient heart
- ✗ *mounds* of sugar and fat parked in or around vital organs
- ✗ Conditions such as diabetes, nervous tension, high blood pressure and cardiovascular disease that are **silently brewing**.

If fitness authorities had it their way, they'd create legislation to make exercise mandatory as soon as a baby leaves the cradle, not during the teenage years when obesity is likely to strike.

But fitness shouldn't be associated with any age limit. You can start at 10 or at 30 – even at 50 and 60 – the idea being that fitness should not be seen as the cure for a condition that's already come about. As the saying goes, don't wait for illness to strike.

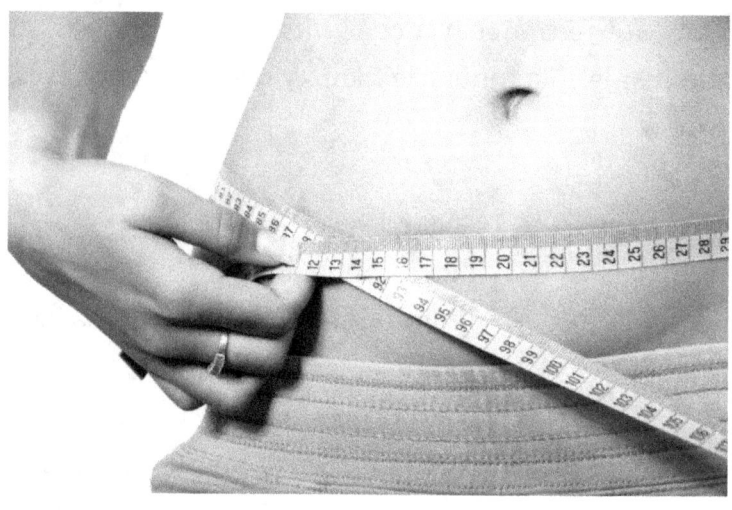

Assessing How Fit You Are

Brad King and Dr. Michael Schmidt in *"Bio Age, Ten Steps to a Younger You"* (Macmillan, Canada, 2001) have devised a questionnaire for assessing physical damage to a body as a result of no exercise. We will borrow some of their guidelines, which we will summarize here:

Start with the question, "**How do I <u>look</u>**?" Do any of these answers apply to you?

> ➤ Am I overweight, looking like an apple or pear?
> ➤ Do I have a spare tire around my waist?
> ➤ Has my skin become excessively dry, almost paper-thin?

Next, ask: "**How do I <u>feel</u>**?"

> ➤ Do my joints hurt before or after any physical exertion?
> ➤ Am I constantly worried and anxious?
> ➤ Do I feel tired and sluggish most of the time?
> ➤ Do I suffer from mood swings?

Last question, "**How am I <u>doing</u>**?"

Are simple walking and climbing stairs difficult?

> ➤ Do I have problems concentrating?

> ➢ Is running impossible for me now?
> ➢ Am I unable to sit straight, preferring to slouch or stoop my shoulders?[1]

You've completed your basic assessment. Note, however, that other exercise or fitness gurus will have their own parameters or indices for assessing your body's overall state and one isn't better than the other.

As long as they include all dimensions of the self – physical, psychological and mental – they are as valid as the next person's assessment charts.

---

[1] Brad J. King & Dr. Michael A. Schmidt. Bio Age – Ten Steps to a Younger You. Macmillan, Canada. 2001.

Greetings!

Who doesn't think they're too busy these days? Let's face it, our society puts so much value on productivity and revenue that some of us find ourselves in a place where we would like to take better care of ourselves but can't seem to find time for it. What is a busy person to do when you want to be able to exercise but think you're too busy to do it?

Here are the facts about transforming yourself into a busy person that has the time to exercise and take care of yourself:

1.   Look at your priorities honestly – if you don't give exercise the priority you give to your job and family, it will remain a wish rather than a reality. You won't be able to be consistent with exercise unless you give it the importance it needs in your life.

2.   Become as good a problem-solver with exercise as you are with your work – for a busy person to be able to exercise regularly they have to use their problem-solving skills to conquer the barriers in their busy lives that keep them from being the active and lean person they want to be.

3.   Schedule exercise like you schedule your meetings, doctor appointments, and other things that you consider commitments. Exercise needs to be a commitment that you respect. If someone asks you to do something during your scheduled exercise time, learn to say, "I'm sorry. I have a commitment then. Let's find another time." You would say it if you had a doctor appointment or meeting at that time. You want to be a busy person AND have time to exercise? Then learn to say, no, when it's your exercise that's at stake.

4.   Avoid conveniences whenever possible – a busy person has to take every opportunity to be active. Take the stairs, walk to talk to someone in the office instead of calling or emailing, get away from your desk periodically to stretch or walk around the office (you can use this time to brainstorm).

5.   Find ways to be active while sitting – do muscle resistance exercises, keep rhythm to music with your body, fidget.

6.   Stop procrastinating – stop repeated complaints to yourself and others about how you want to exercise but don't have time. Confront yourself with the reality that if exercise is what you really want to do, you're going to have to take charge and change some things to accommodate it. Then start focusing to staying consistent with it.

Everything in life takes decision-making and action. Even busy people can be active people. It just takes a little prioritizing, problem-solving, scheduling, and taking advantage of opportunities.

Lavinia Rodriguez, PH.D.

Author of: Mind Over Fat Matters: Conquering Psychological Barriers to Weight Management

website: www.FatMatters.com

"Great Book, Loved it, 2 Thumbs up!" –Troy Bonar MST

Turning You into a Fitness Buff!

After going through the assessment phase, you're probably experiencing what some people fondly call a "rude awakening".

If you're not mentally prepared to accept exercise, please *don't* force yourself. Just be familiar with its benefits and when you're wholeheartedly disposed towards giving it a crack in the can, proceed slowly. "Slowly but surely" is the exercise cult's favorite slogan.

Slowly but Surely...

In fact "slowly but surely" was probably what motivated Denise Austin to come up with her popular one-minute exercises (more on this in a later section).[2] She had two types of people in mind when she designed the one-minute movements:

1. Uninitiated
2. People on the go.

It's a *quickie* society we live in; we want everything quick – **especially exercise!** – and many converts would be willing to include it in their routine for the sake of health, if there were a quick way to get in, and certainly a quick to get out.

---

[2] Denise Austin (with Jerome Agel as producer). Denise Austin's 1-Minute Exercises. Vintage Books/Random House. New York. 1987.

Hi there.

I'm probably just like someone you know. I'm a busy professional and parent. I enjoy relaxing on the couch after a long day and tend to eat lots of snacks while watching T.V. shows and sports. I was fit in my teens and early 20's. However, my couch potato ways got me in trouble as my metabolism changed. I'd skip breakfast, miss lunch, and load up on calories at night. MY WEIGHT AND CHOLESTEROL WENT UP WITH EACH ANNUAL PHYSICAL. I WAS MORE THAN 240 POUNDS BY MY EARLY 30'S!

HOWEVER, I LOST MORE THAN 50 POUNDS WITHOUT DITCHING MY "COUCH POTATO" WAYS! I TRIED OTHER DIET PLANS AND PILLS BUT REGAINED ALL THE WEIGHT AND MORE! I needed an easy plan that fit my lifestyle. I finally found great tasting, more healthful alternatives for comfort foods, snacks, and drinks that fit my lifestyle even pizza, pasta, burgers, cookies, ice cream, chips, candy, coffee, soda, and beer.

I NOW FOLLOW 3 CORE PRINCIPLES IN MY DIET AND LOST MORE THAN 50 POUNDS! PRINCIPLES INCLUDE:

1. ADD MORE PROTEIN/FIBER

2. REDUCE SATURATED FAT/CHOLESTEROL

3. SIGNIFICANTLY REDUCE SUGAR CONSUMPTION

EXERCISE TIP (SOCIAL INCENTIVES AND WALKING)

Do not underestimate the power of social incentives to motivate you to exercise! Humans are social by nature. If you find others that are supportive of your diet and exercise program, you will be more successful. If you can find supportive people to join you... even better! Make diet and exercise a competition and winning becomes a great motivator for success.

Walking is a good first step for exercise. Maybe friends or family members will join you for regular walks in the neighborhood? The easy changes to make are walking instead of driving a cart when playing golf, walking to the local store, taking your pet for a walk, pushing the lawnmower, etc.

Get a pedometer to keep track of your daily steps. This is a cheap and nifty device for your belt to measure the distance you walk for any time period. Use the device to measure your steps today and then set goals to increase steps during your future walks in the neighborhood.

Maybe you can organize a regular walk at work or school with your colleagues? Competition is a great motivator. Have a contest to see which colleague can walk the most steps in a week.

Everyone enjoys social networking websites these days. Did you know you can setup your own exercise group on Facebook™ and link in all your friends, family members, and colleagues? This is a great motivational tool as the group will poke you on-line if you are not participating as regularly.
More tips from my books...

1) ALWAYS START THE DAY WITH BREAKFAST! I recommend eating a high fiber bowl of cereal. Sweeten the bowl with your favorite sugar alternative like the naturally sweet, calorie free stevia. You can also add vanilla soy milk which adds more fiber and protein with heart healthy fats. The extra fiber helps to give you the feeling of a full stomach (and aids the digestive process). The protein helps you to build lean muscle.

2) MAKE YOUR COFFEE AT HOME. You should make your coffee at home to avoid the unhealthy temptations at coffee shops like doughnuts. If you stick with a Columbian blend it will taste great. Always sweeten your cup with your favorite sugar alternative and milk instead of cream (to cut down on carbs and fat). You can stock up on low sugar, high fiber snack bars if you need to eat breakfast on-the-go.

3) HAVE A HEALTHY SNACK BETWEEN BREAKFAST AND LUNCH. I recommend bringing a 100 calorie zip bag with you on-the-go. You can add to the bag your favorite sugar-free cookie like from Josephs Lite Cookies™. These are made with a natural sugar alternative and are half the calories as regular cookies. Bring your healthier snacks with you to the beach!

4) DON'T SKIP LUNCH! Take your lunch with you to work or school. You can make all kinds of easy wraps and sandwiches but always use low-carb or light wheat bread, 99% fat free meats or soy alternatives, and zero calorie condiments like yellow mustard. You can add more zip and flavor to any healthy meal with zero calorie Frank's RedHot™ sauce. Bring your healthier lunch with you to the beach!

5) SNACK BETWEEN LUNCH AND DINNER- the same principle as between breakfast and lunch but switch up the snacks to keep it interesting. You can try peanuts, carrots, soy nuts, celery sticks with peanut-butter, etc. Trader Joes™ soy/corn/flax tortilla chips at 9 net carbs per serving are a great alternative to potato chips.

6) TRY NOT TO EAT A HEAVY DINNER AT NIGHT. You don't want to load up on calories when you are the least active! Try making a two minute smoothie in your blender with 2 scoops of sugar-free vanilla soy protein powder, half of banana, three frozen strawberries, and five packets of your favorite zero calorie sugar alternative like stevia. You can also prepare quick salads from bags and add extra lean, prepackaged chicken or turkey cubes/strips and a light dressing.

7) SNACK AFTER DINNER WHILE WATCHING T.V. You know you can't resist snacking while watching your favorite game, drama, or sitcom. So, why not have a bowl of Edys™ No Sugar Added ice cream with 70% less sugar and 50% less fat? How about a cup of sugar-free and fat-free pudding? I recommend shelled sunflower seeds. You can snack for a long time without taking in many calories as cracking open the shell takes time and you don't actually take in as many seeds.

8) YOU DON'T HAVE TO STOP YOUR DIET WHEN EATING OUT. You can go for the salad bar more often and pick out lean meats, veggies, bacon bits, and add a light dressing. You should leave off the high carb items like croutons. How about doubling up on veggies and leaving the fries off your plate? Why not go for the terriaki chicken skewers instead of the boneless spare ribs and save tons of fat!

9) HAVE A BEER (OR A RUM & DIET SODA IF YOU PLAN TO DRINK A FEW)! You can start out with a heavier beer and then switch to light. If you plan to drink a six pack, drink rum.

10) TAKE ADVANTAGE OF THE WEEKEND TO PREPARE INGREDIENTS FOR QUICK MEALS THROUGHOUT THE WEEK. I bet you like to grill on the weekend and for sports events as most of us do? You can grill up a large package of extra lean chicken or turkey. Cut up the leftovers into cubes and store in the fridge. You can use these cubes to make all kinds of quick sandwiches, wraps, and salads throughout the week. If you make chili, use 99% fat free turkey and freeze the leftovers in 3 cup plastic containers. You can heat these up for any quick lunch or dinner during the busy work week.

THE BOTTOM-LINE FOR STAYING IN SHAPE IS TO EAT REGULAR SMALLER, HEALTHIER MEALS (with higher protein/fiber, lower saturated fat/cholesterol, and significantly lower sugar). This will boost you metabolism. Snacking is fun and satisfying and is an important part of a healthy diet.

- Gregory J.E. Ladas is the author of THE COUCH POTATO DIET. www.thecouchpotatodiet.com
& THE DISCOUNT DIET. WWW.THEDISCOUNTDIET.COM.

Benefits of Exercise

If you make exercise part of your day, Denise Austin believes you'll already experience some noticeable benefits. These include:

- ✓ Waking up in the morning feeling refreshed
- ✓ Walking with a sprightly gait
- ✓ Having energy left at the end of the day
- ✓ Feeling more optimistic about recreation
- ✓ Sleeping more soundly at night

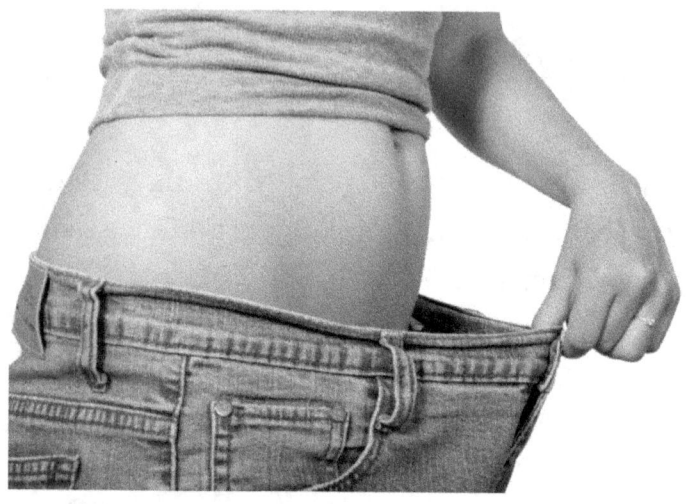

MORE Benefits of Exercise!

The benefits above are general. Let's examine the more specific benefits of exercise on specific parts of the human anatomy, as described by Goldberg and Elliot:

✓ **Exercise prevents heart disease!**

The average ratio of total cholesterol to HDL cholesterol (good cholesterol) is about 4.5. If this ratio doubles or reaches 7, you double your chances of developing coronary heart disease. You reduce that risk by as much as 50% if your ratio is 3 or lower.

The lowdown on cholesterol: not all cholesterol is bad. You have the good one (HDL-1 and HDL-2), the not so bad one (VLDL) and the harmful one (LDL). To get your ratios, divide the total amount of your cholesterol by your amount of HDL. The lower the ratio you have, the better.[3]

✓ **Exercise prevents osteoporosis!**

Ponder the statistics: 28 million Americans have osteoporosis and of this number, 80% are women. Only ¼ of this 80% know they have the condition and only half are being treated. The annual osteoporosis bill to the United States is $14 billion.

Studies have shown that sufficient amounts of calcium and regular exercise build strong bones. While genetics play a major role in developing the risks of osteoporosis, individuals can control some factors that will help prevent the problem.

---

[3] Dr. Lynn Goldberg and Dr. Diane Elliot. The Healing Power of Exercise. John Wiley & Sons. New York. 2000.

Peak bone mass is attained in your 20's. Starting an exercise program while still young, even if you live in the fast lane, will help you avoid this bone disease.

✓ **Exercise prevents diabetes!**

People are still debating how much exercise an individual needs, but for people with type 2 diabetes, exercising three or more times a week improves fitness and blood sugar levels. If you have type 2 diabetes and are overweight, exercise done with the following parameters would be of tremendous benefit: intensity of 60%-70% maximal heart rate, with duration of 30 or more minutes, 4-7 days each week.[4]

The above benefits are only a *few* of the many advantages that an exercise/fitness regimen will provide.

There have been hundreds of documented reports that reveal how people's lives have significantly

----

[4] Goldberg and Elliot.

improved and the remarkable transformation that their bodies experience after they made the decision to take ownership of their weight and fat problems.

In fact, Diane Rinehart (former Toronto magazine editor and writer) wrote in the Montreal Gazette on December 12, 2005:

> **"What we're hearing about...is waiting times in emergency and operating rooms for ailments such as hip replacements, heart surgery and amputations. That's a shame because the fact is, if we dealt with obesity, we wouldn't be facing the epidemics of heart disease, stroke, arthritis and diabetes that clog our hospital waiting rooms and OR's."[5]**

---

[5] Newspaper article. "The Cutting-the-Fat Issue that Politicians Ignore." Montreal Gazette. Dec. 12, 2005.

With a full time job (lawyer) with a new book, (listed below) I needed an exercise regimen that takes no time to start to do. Thus, I walk daily, whether travelling or getting to work early so that I fit the walk in or wherever I may be.

I am fanatical about fitting my half hour to hour walk in, even if it means marching in place for at least a half an hour. This keeps the metabolism humming and makes a lifelong change in ones life guaranteed to make one more fit, thinner and happier.

Ellen Pober Rittberg
 "35 Things Your Teen Wont Tell You So I Will"
www.ellenpoberrittberg.com
erittberg@gmail.com
twitter: ellen_rittberg tumblr:
ellenpoberrittberg.tumblr.com

2

Section 2: No Matter How Busy You Are, there are Ways You *CAN* Include Exercise

Feeling overwhelmed by the amount of time your friends and colleagues spend in the gym? Turned off by the idea of a tennis game that entails not only the hour-long match but also getting to the tennis club, changing into a tennis outfit and then showering afterwards?

You think, "That's almost 3 hours – three hours I could devote to nurturing my clients and expanding my sales territory!" The bad news is, being penny wise and pound foolish does not work in ANY circumstance, especially where fitness and health are concerned.

Are those three hours worth skipping during a given week when you know that **years** of optimum health can be yours if you had a positive attitude accompanied by reasonable doses of discipline?

Fitness & Health for the Busy Professional

Hi!

I am Susan Schenck, the author of the 2-time award-winning book, 'The Live Food Factor: The Comprehensive Guide to the Ultimate Diet for Body, Mind, Spirit & Planet'. My book (which hit no. 23 in all genres at amazon.com in January 2009) has gained the reputation as the raw foods encyclopedia or bible. I have been a guest on dozens of radio shows, including The Frankie Boyer Show, Your Time with Kim Iverson, and The Sharon Kleyne Hour. You can also view me making some raw recipes on local TV at www.livefoodfactor.com. I also have a master's degree and license in Chinese medicine.

The best thing for people to have for lunch to boost their energy is a green smoothies. The greens provide oxygen to increase work productivity. The greens make the person more alkaline instead of acidic, which is draining. I have come home on a Friday night, exhausted after a 60-hour work week, made myself a green smoothie containing fresh squeezed orange juice and kale and a pinch of cayenne, and have been suddenly energized enough to clean my condo!

Here is a recipe: 1/2 bunch kale leaves, chopped, with 1/2 cup fresh fruit juice (juice from 2 oranges) Blend in blender, preferably a heavy duty one so that it is creamy and not flakey. Add a pinch of cayenne if you like.

TV TIP:
While watching TV, jump on a mini trampoline for half an hour, which cleanses your lymph nodes. Another way to do that is jumping rope, but since the trampoline is more fun, you are more likely to stick with it.

Health,
Susan Schenck, LAC
Cuenca, Ecuador

A Simple Exercise Program

Instead of *ignoring* exercise altogether, here's a suggestion for integrating it into your busy schedule. Think of exercise like you think of a major task in the office. Break it up into tinier components.

Instead of spending two hours in the gym or in the tennis court like your friends do, ask your trainer to divide your workout program.

Suggestion A

30 minutes four times a week, i.e.: 20 minutes cardio, 10 minutes weights (1 muscle group, e.g. legs)

Suggestion B

30 minutes three times a week
Mon: 20 minutes cardio + 10 minutes stretching;
Tues: 20 minutes weights (2 muscle groups, e.g. back and abdominals) + 10 minutes of cardio.

Wed: 20 minutes cardio + 10 minutes of Weights (two muscle groups, e.g. triceps or chest, biceps or shoulders)

Suggestion C

20 minutes 5 days a week.

Week 1: all cardio

Week 2: weights

Week 3: Cardio on Mon/Wed/Fri

Week 4: Weights on Tues/Thurs

Repeat the entire cycle when you get to month 2.

Troy,

I'm a husband, 54 year old father of 2 teenagers and a pre-teen. Besides that, I am a Founding Director of an International Consulting firm, and I do a significant amount of volunteer work.

I used to go to the gym 3 times a week before I was married, and I was buff. Once I was married, and especially after becoming a father, I couldn't spare time for the gym.

Due to heredity and thinking that I was bulletproof when I was younger, I am now being treated for the typical conditions caused by our stressful/sedentary lifestyle (cholesterol, blood pressure, heart rhythm). I've reached the age where the majority of drug commercials on TV apply to me, and I'm taking at least one drug in each class. Then, there are a few chronic conditions that have settled in over the last 10 years.

All of my doctors told me that my conditions would improve with exercise. (My endocrinologist said I didn't have to exercise--only if I wanted to live.)

I needed to find a way to exercise that would keep me motivated and wouldn't take up time I needed for the family or work. I turned to cycling. I now cycle to the office and back almost every day. I stay motivated, because I have to get to the office and we sold our second car. Once at the office, I have to cycle to get home. I get 45 minutes of aerobic activity 5 days a week, cycling a total of 50 miles during the typical week.

Cycling uses the time I would have spent commuting some other way. Driving to work took 15-20 minutes one way; cycling takes me 20-25 minutes one way. On bad days, I work out all my frustrations cycling home, so our home life is more peaceful.

I can carry shirts, slacks, and underwear on my bike, and I deliver suits to my office over the weekend. Showering at home just before cycling to work, and drinking plenty of clear water on the way, means that I only need to towel off at the office when I change from cycling jerseys and shorts to street clothes. I shower again when I get home, and that washes away the last bit of worry that should have stayed at the office.

Frequency and Intensity

Ideally, one should gradually increase the frequency or intensity, or both. But if you're busy, and definitely can't spare more than 30 minutes a day, then increase your intensity. This means if your cardio involves the treadmill, take the notch up 1 level (if you started with level 3, go on to level 4 on month 2).

For your weight training, if you started with 5-pound weights, graduate into 7.5 pounds in month

2. And then on those days when your day is not filled with meetings, try to stay an extra 5-10 minutes.

Be realistic with your goals, especially when you're just starting. Increasing frequency and intensity too soon can overwhelm you, making you want to give up.

Variety is the Spice of Life

Another way to integrate exercise into a busy schedule is to vary the fitness routine. Variety promotes interest in maintaining your workout schedule. Without variety, boredom sets in, causing you to drop out.

Variety also enables you to accommodate as many different types of exercises from the wide repertory available from personal trainers, books and manuals – and the Internet – and that way you're able to adopt certain movements that you're most comfortable with.

Master Troy

An effortless way that busy professionals can stay fit is for them to Count their Steps. It is simple, before taking a bite, they should check out how many steps* it takes to burn off the calories from some of their favorite foods.

The information below is courtesy of www.globalfit.com , a leading provider of benefits for healthy living. GlobalFit is readily accessible to employees through their employers and insurers. GlobalFit's "Destination: You," program breaks new ground by combining step-based activity -- effortlessly verifiable through cutting-edge technology -- with education, community support and incentives to motivate large populations.

One serving of mashed potatoes - 1540 steps
One serving of chocolate ice cream - 1980 steps
Macaroni and cheese- 2640 steps
Large french fries- 6000
Slice of pepperoni pizza - 4560
Cheeseburger - 3840
Doughnut - 2640
Chocolate-chip cookie - 2520
Milk chocolate bar- 2520
16 potato chips - 1800
Mug of beer - 1680
Can of cola - 1680
4 cups of buttered popcorn - 1488
10 thin pretzels - 1320
Banana - 1068
Hardboiled egg - 936
Navel orange - 828
14 baby carrots - 672
*Steps based on average calorie burn for a 150-pound person.

Best, Nancy Hite-Norde

Walk before you Run...

If you're an <u>absolute beginner</u>, a full blown workout which incorporates cardio, weights, and flexibility may scare or discourage you. The idea is to start with small steps.

Do one exercise segment at a time (refer to our suggestions, item 2 above). Besides, very few people can accomplish a two-hour workout more than once or twice a week.

Another way of doing it would be to integrate your favorite sport (swimming, cycling or walking) during the week and say, a particular activity like yoga which doesn't necessitate jumping into the car and making a dash for the washrooms before cardio classes start.

With yoga for example, all you need is a mat and a quiet room in your house for about 20 minutes.

The Book
ADDICTED TO STRESS is an excellent resource, I highly recommend it! I also recommend visiting the site: http://www.turnonyourinnerlight.com/page7.html
This site is full of great resources for everything fitness related! There was so much content that Debbie offered us for this project, we could not get it all in. When I went to the site I realized how much value she brings to people's lives
 -Troy Bonar

DEBBIE MANDEL, M.A. is an Author/Radio Host/Websites Host/Speaker/Fitness and Stress Management Expert

Her books include:

Addicted to Stress: A Woman's 7 Step Program to Reclaim Joy and Spontaneity in Life

Turn On Your Inner Light: Fitness for Body, Mind and Soul

Changing Habits: The Caregivers' Total Workout

http://www.turnonyourinnerlight.com/index.html

Time Management

If your schedule gets you up and running beginning at 9 in the morning until six in the evening, this day represents 9 hours. There are 24 hours a day and we're not recommending you get up at 2 in the morning to do your exercise.

But have you ever thought that if you get up at 7 to be ready for 9, maybe you can set your alarm clock 45 minutes earlier, using these 45 minutes to engage in a physical activity? If you do this three times a week, that means you get 135 minutes that you can allocate for exercise.

One easy way to do this is to do yoga in the morning (it requires only a mat and comfortable, loose clothing), or turn on a fitness CD/DVD, or buy a treadmill (the foldable ones) that you can jump into as soon as you wake up.

Master Troy,

The thing about being in shape is that shortcuts don't really work. I tried for years to run when I had time, watch what I ate, cut back on calories here, take the stairs there, walk the dog longer, and make other smart choices, but I kept slowly gaining weight through my early thirties. I've been an active martial artist most of my life and am a high energy person, but still, my clothes were getting tighter. One day when my niece was playfully joking about my growing posterior, I decided that was enough. Despite not having time for it, I went with a friend to the gym, got a membership and dedicated myself to doing what I needed to do to get healthy. What I needed to do was work out 5-6 days very hard, dramatically reduce fatty foods, and cut back on portion sizes. This has changed my entire life. Instead of waking up early to work, I began getting up for 5:30 and 5:45 a.m. classes at the gym.

This means I have to go to bed at a decent hour, cut back on alcohol so I'm not dehydrated for the morning's workout and make many more changes that have impacted pretty much every facet of my life. But it's paid off. I am down 6 sizes and am still getting complimented regularly on how much healthier and slimmer I look.

My schedule is hectic. I work very long hours many days, plus I teach jujitsu and am active in my church. But I've made my health a priority and it has shown in other aspects of my life. The biggest advice I can impart is to make it a priority and schedule accordingly. Early morning workouts are best for active people. Once you get into the rhythm, it's really not that difficult to maintain. Going to classes has really helped me because I know there are people there waiting for me.

Becky Sheetz-Runkle,
Vice President, Client Services
Author of Sun Tzu for Women and co-founder of Q2
Marketing. (www.q2marketing.com)

VISIT THE TECHNOLOGY MARKETING BLOG

Q2 Marketing

Follow Becky at twitter.com/BeckySheetz

Another time management tip: not only do busy managers have back-to-back meetings, they also have luncheon and dinner meetings to meet with clients. Assess each client. Do all of them really need to be wined and dined? Is an hour long meeting absolutely necessary? Can't a deal be negotiated on the phone?

See how many meetings you can cancel or shorten. Then fit your fitness program into those slots that have been freed up.

How about this suggestion: instead of going to lunch with clients every day of the week, why don't you schedule lunch meetings for say Monday and Tuesday? This way you can incorporate a fitness routine for Wednesday, Thursday and Friday from 12:00 to 1:00 pm.

A brisk walk inside or outside the office building, a quick swim in the neighborhood hotel, a Pilates course in the recreational centre, lifting dumb bells while on the phone?

Any of these exercises is better than no exercise. Your guiding principle should be to move, move, move as frequently as you can manage it.

Hello Troy! Here are some things that have helped me.

I tend to get up early, like 5 a.m. and get out and walk! I can get in about 6,000 steps in an hour. Especially in the summer I'll keep fresh peaches, nectarines, figs, etc. on the counter so I can grab something to eat throughout the day. During the day, I select one exercise or movement that I can do 100 reps with... say, squats. Before eating anything, I'll do 10-25 reps of the movement. This gets my digestive system working. Then I eat but never more than what will stop me from doing another set of movement IF I wanted to.

If you work outside the home, find a route that will take about 15 minutes to do and do it before eating, that way you're sure to get it done. If there are stairs there, use them whenever possible. Keep flat shoes available.

Always keep apples available to munch on. They are filling and filled with nutrition. Keep a smoothie in a thermos. Make a full blender and divide into thirds. One for before or on the way to work; the second is good for lunch and the third for on the way home so you'll eliminate the after work hunger and not stop off at a fast food joint or scrounge through the cupboards after getting home looking for anything and everything. Once home, eat and apple, get in some movement, then have your evening meal ~ if you still want it.

Revvell P. Revati
http://BodaciousLiving.com
Intentional Self-Mastery

Just as ergonomic experts are recommending to office workers to take their eyes off their computer screen every hour or so, fitness experts are advocating getting up from your chair and taking a walk and jaunting up and down the stairs.

When you feel the need to take a break, offer to pick up supplies for your colleagues, take the mail downstairs instead of waiting for the trolley, or think of something you could put in your car instead of waiting until 5 pm. That way, you force yourself to get up from your seat and walk for a few minutes.

Fitness & Health for the Busy Professional

If you look into the private offices of some people, you'll see dumb bells, mats and elastic bands – these are clues that they are doing some exercise while on the job – a good and healthy practice to adopt by busy individuals with hectic schedules.

Hi Troy,

I provided both of my employees with gym membership. These two women were good friends as well as co-workers. So every day after work they would go to the gym and workout together. One of the women quit and my other employee stopped going to the gym. She had a husband and a couple of kids and suddenly just didn't have the time for it anymore. So when it came time to give her a raise, I gave her a choice: either cash or 3 hours a week paid for going to the gym. She took the gym credit and said it was the best raise she ever got. I told her she had to treat that time religiously; no running errands or doing something else, she had to go to the gym. Well, that was two years ago and she has lost 65 lbs and kept it off. She seems less stressed and is incredibly loyal. She eats a lot better than she did in the past; she's embraced a total wellness approach. Let me know if you would like to speak to her and I can provide you with her email address. Thanks Troy. I know this isn't really a diet tip, but maybe you can use it.

Bonnie Lee, E.A.

www.twitter.com/BLTaxpertise
www.taxpertise.com
Symmetry Business Services
P. O. Box 1401
Boyes Hot Springs, CA 95416

Fitness & Health for the Busy Professional
Family Exercises

On the weekends when you join the family in their activities, try to integrate exercise into these activities: if the children are into cycling, join them for bike rides. Are they off to their swimming lessons or skating lessons? See if you can sign up in the adults section, or take a walk outside the recreational center while waiting for them.

Everyday men and women come home and face the arduous task of figuring out the answer to the dinner dilemma. "What will I make for dinner tonight?" It makes it really easy after a long day, to just give in to the temptation to run through the drive through if you don't already have a plan in place for losing weight and what to do for dinner. That's where E-mealz comes in. E-Mealz relies on a team of experienced meal planners, writers and editors to create new menus every week that are designed around grocery store sales, seasonal specials and diet preferences. Diet preferences include Weight Watchers, low fat, and vegetarian to name a few. For $5.00 per month, subscribers download a recipe plan online for the week with a matching aisle-by-aisle grocery list. The easy-to-follow recipes usually contain fewer than seven ingredients to allow for prep times of less than 30 minutes. We have been spoken of highly already in this regard in the Redbook February 2010 issue. One Red Book reader slimmed down from a size 20 to a size 10 with the help of E-mealz!

Heather Brown
Product Development & Marketing
E-mealz Inc   www.E-mealz.com

Chores Burn Calories!

Who says you can't burn calories while doing housework or gardening? Take a breather from your hectic schedule and devote some down time to tending to your lawn, trimming your rose bushes, scrubbing the kitchen and bathroom floors, etc.

Light household chores : 439 calories per hour.

Yard work: 500 calories per hour.

Source (caloriecount.com)

Troy's FAT Bank Book Plug #1:

I have a special book for people who do not or can not exercise very well and still want to lose weight, THE FAT BANK. It talks about how to lose hundreds of pounds without adding exercise until you are ready and able. Available soon at www.thefatbank.com.

*Also check out the last part of this book it contains the **secret** to weight loss.*

Walk, don't Drive!

And here's another tip that is popular: park your car far away so you can walk to the front gates of the office, to the entrance of the mall, to the doctor's office and to the post office.

Greetings Master Troy!

I own a very busy mental health counseling practice; I have three grown children, all of whom married in a ten-month period of time last year. At the same time, my first book (www.eatitupbook.com) was published and I have been traveling around the country speaking at conferences. My ailing mother also lives with my husband and myself. I have a top-of-the-line elliptical at my office and a great treadmill at home, along with hand weight.

Almost without exception, I do a 30 - 60 minute workout five times a week, no matter how late it is or how tired I am, using the mantra "It's what I do" to deter any excuses I could easily come up with to forego the exercise. The workout not only keeps me in shape, it helps keep me sane!

--
Connie Stapleton, Ph.D.
Office:706-364-5228
Fax: 706-364-5229
www.mindbodyhealthservices.com
www.eatitupbook.com
cstapletonphd@mindbodyhealthservices.com

3

Section 3: Busy Traveler? You Can Fit Exercise into your Trips!

Hopping in and out of planes is exercise enough, you say. But that's not the kind of exercise that will condition your heart, make your reflexes and joints more fluid, keep the sugar levels or keep you from swinging from one mood to another!

Nor is it the kind of exercise that will make you euphoric after a good cardiovascular session. You need to counteract the effects of jet lag, artificial air in pressurized aircraft cabins and sky fatigue. Suzanne Schlosberg says,

"Sometimes your travels help you recognize how humdrum your workout routine has become. At home, it's easy to fall into a rut – to use the same weight machines in the same order, week after week, month after month, simply out of habit. But a trip may take the routine out of your routine. You may have no choice but to try new strength exercises or jog in the pool instead of swim laps. And you might find these new pursuits so enjoyable that you add them to your fitness repertoire at home."[6]

---

[6] Suzanne Schlosberg. The Ultimate Workout Guide for the Road. Houghton Mifflin Co. Boston, USA. 2002.

Hello Troy,
 Three years ago I signed up for a program called Heal Your Hunger (www.HealYourHunger.com) that changed my life and my waist line. I was 60 pounds overweight and abused unhealthy behaviors. I was a busy women - I worked in treatment centers and private practice with people with eating disorders and addictions (as a doctor of psychology) but had my own issues personally. Leading the double life was killing me and the stress from over-working to escape the pain was the worst part of all! I was exhausted and used food, sugar, and addictions to continue "doing, doing doing" when the natural steam and energy would wear off.

I overworked to escape the terrible emotional pain I was in, but Heal Your Hunger helped me to change my life to be able to stop running from myself and stop using food and unhealthy behaviors and addictions. I maintained my job and continued living at home and attending social functions while receiving mentorship to be able to change my life from the inside out (from living in it while receiving their care). That is how I received effortless weight loss and freedom from unhealthy behaviors. That was three and a half years ago and the weight loss and freedom has sustained over time. This is the most incredible gift for the successful business person or parent with absolutely no extra time. Through going through this process I actually felt that there was 'more'time and what I did do with my time was more productive. I hope this is helpful for you. If you have any questions about my experience or the process I went through to heal, please let me know. Thank you. All good wishes to you,

Dr. Talia Witkowski

Common Obstacles

What are some of the reasons why travelers do not incorporate exercise while they're on the road?

- ⇨ They're stressed or too tired
- ⇨ They don't feel comfortable about working out in unfamiliar surroundings
- ⇨ They don't have access to a hotel gym

But if they made just a tiny effort to change this thinking, they'd be on the road to fitness sooner.

Engaging in exercise allows you to get out of that bubble of meetings, seminars and tours.

Troy's Insight: You will probably never see the people at the hotel again, so it is a great place for you to work out. You would be amazed at some of the connections that can be made at the hotel Gym. If anyone else does show up, they are probably in the same situation as you.

Automatically you have a common interest. Maybe the person sees you working out and they are in your meeting the next day, this shows them that you are committed to your success and automatically gains their respect.

TROY'S TIP-
Shower Time Push-ups or sit ups- Do as many as you can before getting into the shower then after you shower and dry off, do as many as you can again.

You will be amazed how much you can build up with this simple 1 or 2 minutes in the morning while at home or on the road.

When traveling, have a pair of good walking shoes (trainers preferably) so that you won't feel so daunted about getting from one side of the airport to another.

Having the right pair of walking shoes will encourage you to walk up the stairs instead of take the escalator, to walk instead of taking the conveyor belt, and to transfer from one concourse to another on foot instead of taking the shuttle service.

You may not know it, but walking these long distances with your luggage in tow serves as a combination/weight lifting exercise!

Fitness & Health for the Busy Professional

Greetings, Samurai of Success!

I am very busy with speaking, writing, and coaching and also raising a family. I will grab little pockets of time to keep fit. I walk whenever I get the chance, even if it is only for a few minutes. I stretch throughout the day.

I make exercise appointments with myself and commit to that time. This is huge--it has to be as important as any other important **appointment. in** your life. Instead of sitting and talking on the weekend, which is also nice, my husband and I will catch up on things while we walk together.
I drink lots of water and get enough sleep. All of these things help me stay healthy and in shape. Hope this helps!

Diana Fletcher

         Diana Fletcher Life Coaching

Author of Reduce Your Stress, Month by Month Stress Reducing Strategies

Stress-Reducing Expert Coach,
Speaker, and Author of the Outstanding Life Series, Co-Author of Inspired Entrepreneurs
              www.dianafletcher.com
Book Diana to Speak!

Once settled comfortably on the plane, make sure you time your stretching and walking periods. If it's just an hour's flight, walk around the plane once and do your stretching at the back of the plane; if it's a three hour to five hour flight (east to west in the North American continent), try to get up from your seat and walk around at least once every hour, doing leg extensions and trunk/neck movements.

If you're crossing the Pacific or Atlantic oceans, those killer flights need not kill you. Increase the frequency of your stretches and walking.

Airlines such as Japan Air Lines show videos of how travelers can incorporate flexibility movements while seated or standing. Take full advantage of these videos. The exercises may help you ward off fatigue and jet lag.

A note about DVT

In the last five years, there have been reports about flight passengers, especially in economy class, suffering from DVT – deep vein thrombosis.

The link between confining airplane seats and deaths from DVT (formation of deadly blood clots) has been established by the United Nations World Health Organization. It has nothing to do with gender, risk factors or genetics. Everyone is at risk in economy class![7]   This should constitute

---

[7] Hwww.brightlife.com

compelling reason to integrate exercise while high in the sky.

To make exercise possible while traveling, schedule your flights so that when you get to your destination, you don't rush through dinner and then go to sleep.

Try to arrive during the late afternoon/early evening, to give you time to shake off the fatigue from the trip, and have at least an hour to do exercises either in your hotel room or in the hotel gym.

Hi Troy,
I've included some tips below from our client, prominent Los Angeles-based personal trainer and life coach, Dennis Grounds.

"Maintaining a fitness regime while during your busy schedule can be challenging, however it does not need to take a lot of time. Here are three main actions to take when things get hectic.

1) STRUCTURE: Look at your schedule and pencil in 30 minutes for working out. Putting your workout in your schedule just as you would your business meetings. In this 30 min you can do interval training which is a combination of cardio and resistant training. Make your 30 min focused and nonstop.

2) CITY WALK: Go for a walk/run at the end of your day in the city you are in. This is a good way to burn some calories and get out of the office.

3) STAIRS: If the building you work in has more than 1 floor, find the emergency stair case and go up and down the stairs several times. This is great cardio and leg workout. From a nutritional perspective, and given that lunches and dinners are often an afterthought during a busy day, here are some practical tips for staying within a sane calorie range each day.

Remember the **P.A.C.E. YOURSELF** guideline.

P stands for PORTION control. Eat half of what you are being served on your plate.

A stands for ALCOHOL. Keep alcohol intake to one drink at dinner. Remember alcohol is considered a carbohydrate and there are a lot of hidden calories in mixed drinks.

C stands for CUT your COMPLEX CARBS such as bread, potatoes, pasta. Complex carbs causes our insulin level to increase when we ingest them thus making it harder for our metabolism to use fat as fuel.

E stands for EAT fresh vegetables. Veggies are high in vitamins and minerals and low in caloric value. Eat as much as you want. They make a great snack too.

If you follow the **P.AC.E guideline** you are sure to keep caloric range down w/out having to count calories.

A few tips for slipping fitness activities into a hectic day?

GOOD MORNING 10 minutes! When you wake up first thing, (okay, second thing. Coffee first.) take 10 minutes to stretch, do some push ups, jog in place or any type of physical movement in your room. Doing this it gets rid of any stagnant energy and gets your heart rate up, therefore bringing more oxygen into your lungs, increasing your energy for the day.

If you can find 10 minutes in other parts of your day, perhaps while you are on a break, walk, move around, be active. Remember just because you're schedule is busy does not mean you have to put your health and well being on hold. You just get to be more creative and give your body something new and different to try.

Why is it important to not shelve your fitness routine just because you're on the road? Often we use our "very busy schedule" as an excuse not to work out. The truth is time is an invented conversation we are having with ourselves. Time is eternity! Either we manage our time or time will manage us. It is important to view your workouts as a lifestyle behavior vs. a "have to!"

Keeping yourself going on the road has just as many benefits as it does when you are not traveling. Think about it! Less stress, better sleep, reductions in calories and you increase the good endorphins in your brain so you feel better. Who doesn't want that?

---- Dennis Grounds is a personal trainer and life coach, and creator of Training Grounds for Life. Grounds is one of the most sought after trainers in Los Angeles, combining cardio circuit, functional and core training, Pilates and certified life coaching. Training Grounds for Life is an exclusive, luxury studio in Los Angeles where Grounds gets to the "core" of the matter, helping clients to strengthen the core of their bodies as well as the core of their minds.

www.traininggroundsforlife.com

Important "to do" things when traveling

- ✓ Be fully rested before a trip – have the usual "to pack" items ready well in advance so you're not scampering for them at the last minute, depleting your energy levels.

- ✓ Time your sleep correctly – as soon as you board, get the local time of your destination and set your watch accordingly. If it's already night time in your destination, wear blindfolds and ask for a pillow and try to catch a few winks.

- ✓ Drink plenty of water – wine and cocktails will only dehydrate you further; note that humidity levels inside aircraft is below 10%, so water is your best bet.

Fitness & Health for the Busy Professional

Greetings!

I tend to get up early, like 5 a.m. and get out and walk! I can get in about 6,000 steps in an hour. Especially in the summer I'll keep fresh peaches, nectarines, figs, etc. on the counter so I can grab something to eat throughout the day. During the day, I select one exercise or movement that I can do 100 reps with. For example, squats. Before eating anything, I'll do 10-25 reps of the movement. This gets my digestive system working. Then I eat but never more than what will stop me from doing another set of movement IF I wanted to.

If you work outside the home, find a route that will take about 15 minutes to do and do it before eating, that way you're sure to get it done. If there are stairs there, use them whenever possible. Keep flat shoes available.

Always keep apples available to munch on. They are filling and filled with nutrition. Keep a smoothie in a thermos. Make a full blender and divide into thirds. One for before or on the way to work; the second is good for lunch and the third for on the way home so you'll eliminate the after work hunger and not stop off at a fast food joint or scrounge through the cupboards after getting home looking for anything and everything. Once home, eat and apple, get in some movement, then have your evening meal ~ if you still want it.

Revvell P. Revati

http://BodaciousLiving.com Intentional Self-Mastery

Fitness & Health for the Busy Professional

If your job requires you to travel at least four times a month, ask your company's travel department to book you in hotels with gyms or a swimming pool.

Make time out of your travel schedule to insert a workout into your grinding schedule.

Here's a friendly suggestion: get up earlier in the morning and before or after breakfast, head over to the gym and do a brisk walk on the treadmill for 10 minutes, or do the rowing machine (great for the core muscles, back problem reliever) for 10 minutes.

This session is just to wake you up from your travel stupor. See if you can walk to your business appointment instead of taking a cab (that's another 10 minutes).

Hi!

Planning is the key to staying healthy while busy! I run two businesses and still make time to workout everyday and eat healthy. While convince foods may be more expensive, if they are going to allow you to eat more fruits and vegetables, they are worth the extra money. I make a big batch of brown rice, beans, and cut up vegetables and fruits every Sunday. When I need a quick family dinner, I just grab the prepared produce and gains and get cooking.

Thanks,

Alex Caspero MA, RD
Exercise Physiologist
Registered Dietitian
Owner, Delicious Knowledge
www.delicious-knowledge.com
www.facebook.com/deliciousknowledge

At night before going to bed, go to the hotel gym again and lift weights for 10 minutes, to complete your workout for the day. This way you did your cardio and resistance training, two essential components of a fitness program.

Now, tell us, doesn't a 10-20 minute session sound less intimidating than clocking 1.5 hours in the gym?

Hello Troy,

When I'm busy and life has taken over, I have to look at what I did right instead of what I did wrong when it comes to my health. There are a few simple ways to gain some wellness points during your day. Here are a few to aim to practice each day.

- Start your day with breakfast. The earlier your metabolism starts, the longer it runs during the day.

- Park your car far away from the office door. You'll get a few more hundred steps and a few less door dings! Double-whammy!

- Take the stairs...up and down. This will raise your heart rate for a few minutes and you'll start to feel the burn in your legs. Hello, beautiful calves!

- If you're sitting at a desk all day, get up at least every 1-2 hours to go to the bathroom, get water, or just to stand up. Move your body.

- Eat at least 2 fruits and 2 vegetables a day. I know this is below the recommendations, but 2 is a more realistic goal. These small steps lead to big steps.

- If you drink milk, make it fat-free. If you eat bread, make it whole-grain. If you eat pasta, make it whole-wheat. If you eat cereal, use a measuring cup. If you drink soda, drink only one.

- Brush your teeth for 2 minutes and move the whole time. Try doing squats for 2 minutes while brushing or pace your bathroom floor.

- Watch your favorite TV show, but try to get up and do something during each commercial break.

- While making phone calls, walk around your home.

- Laugh. Laughing keeps you sane and healthy!

To your Health!!

Brooke Worley M.S.
Health Promotion--University of Kentucky

Account Representative
www.MyFoodDiary.com
651 Perimeter Drive, Suite 620
Lexington, KY 40515

Aligned Web Solutions, Inc.

Working out with Friends

Another friendly suggestion: if you're traveling in a group, ask a colleague if he or she would do a game of squash or tennis with you. The concierge can give you local addresses of sports or recreational centers in the vicinity.

Hi, My name is D. Lauren O'Connor. I'm a Registered Dietitian. BELOW are some tips for busy folks. Also check out some tips I put together specifically for busy moms: http://nutrisavvysblog.wordpress.com/2009/11/17/balancing-nutrition-and-your-baby/

1. PLAN AHEAD: Prepare lunch/snacks the evening before or use Sunday to prep non-perishable snacks such as a handful of mixed nuts and dried fruits. Apples and bananas are some of nature's most portable energy sources. If choosing an energy bar: look for whole food ingredients, rather than additives, chemicals and excess sugars. A good rule of thumb for these bars is 3+ grams fiber/5+ grams protein to provide sustaining energy. Remember fiber and protein are key. Since they take longer to digest, these will help keep you satisfied so you don't go back for multiple helpings.

2. SCHEDULE TIME TO EAT: Work within your allotted breaks to ensure you get the proper nutrition. A balanced diet with plenty of fresh fruits and vegetables is important. If you must eat on the go, be conscious of what you are putting in your mouth. Mindless munching will add calories, and potential weight gain. Prevent overindulgence by taking the time to chew your food. This will also prevent bloating, gas, upset stomach.

3.HIT THE SALAD BAR OR BRING YOUR OWN: This will ensure plenty of fruit and vegetable intake. Choose green leafy varieties such as romaine, arugulas and spinach for the base. Top with crunchy vegetables such as cucumbers, celery, jicama, bell pepper for added texture/variety and to slow your eating. Top with healthy proteins such as low-fat cottage cheese, skinless chicken or grilled/poached fish. Add color and variety with avocado slices, tomatoes, mushrooms, etc. A few nuts (5-10) can add a tastey, crunchy element to your meal and add healthful antioxidants/vitamins such as walnuts (omega 3's) or almonds (vitamin E). Dressing on the side (a vinaigrette is best) is recommended to ensure your otherwise healthy salad is not drenched with added fat and calories. Add it sparingly or dip lightly as you go.

These are just a few tips... hope it helps. :)

When there's no Gym!

If the hotel gym is crowded or "temporarily closed for maintenance," you can still exercise – in the comfort of your room.

Here are some exercises that you can perform:

- ✓ Turn on the TV or sound system and jog in place; or look up the TV guide and see if some fitness shows are on, or get a fitness video to play in your laptop.

- ✓ Jog in place or jump rope (great cardiovascular workout)

- ✓ Conduct floor exercises (described below)

Hello!

NME (tm) (No More Excuses) Fitness is a quick 15-minute workout that Fran Harris created for her executive women clients. It's four 15-minute workouts a day to stay alert, healthy and fit. The athlete picks four items from a menu of about 100 items: arms, abs, breathing and stretching. They commit to one for 15 minutes throughout the day. Because it's a quick commitment Fran knows two things: (1) they'll do it and (2) it will render maximum results because they are not rushing to get to another thing. When they lay their heads down at night, Fran knows they've gotten a focused, results-oriented workout.

Connect with Fran: http://franharristv.com

Become A Fan: http://facebook.com/franharristv

Follow Fran: http://twitter.com/franharris

Watch FranTV weekdays @ 10 am CST
http://franharriscoaching.com

- **Floor exercise 1**: the Cobra (or back extension). Lying on your stomach as though getting ready for push-ups, keep your hands on your side with palms facing down and fingers pointed forward. With your hands, push to lift your torso off the floor (ensure you're lifting head, shoulders and chest only).

Keep pelvis on the floor and your head looking ahead. Hold and then release. Repeat 3 times. You should feel your spine lengthen. Joe Decker recommends not just pressing back with your hands, but also pushing your upper body up and forward.

Do not tilt your head back to look at the ceiling (many people make this mistake). This puts a strain on your neck.[8]

- **Floor exercise 2**: Crunch (for lower abdominals). The lower abdominals are the weakest muscles in your torso because they are rarely worked, and they're the first to sag after childbirth and after menopause.

---

[8] Joe Decker. The World's Fittest You. Penguin Group. USA. 2004.

This exercise will help:

> Lying flat on your back with your knees bent, cross your arms over your chest. Squeeze your buttocks, tighten your abdomen and push your lower back into the floor. Hold for 10-20 seconds, breathing normally. Relax, and then release. Repeat as often as you can, without overworking yourself.[9]

- **Floor exercise 3**: Hurdler's Stretch. Bend the knee towards the front, and then tuck your lower leg in toward the opposite thigh. Stretch gently toward the straight leg. Do not bounce. This movement is like the ballet movement when an arm goes above the head gracefully, which stretches the sides of the trunk to increase flexibility.[10]

---

[9] Alisa Bauman, Sari Harrar and the editors of Prevention Health Books. Fat to Trim at any Age. Rodale Press. USA. 1998.
[10] Denise Austin.

Fitness & Health for the Busy Professional

If you pick up any exercise book, there will be a rich inventory of exercises you can perform while on the go. Pack this in your bag so you can refer to it for correct form and posture.

Greetings!

I've found that high intensity interval style workouts are best for my hectic schedule but they do require some serious effort. I'm very busy and something like alternating sets of heavy squats and bench press, and then walking lunges and pull-ups only takes 30 minutes or so and is a killer workout.

Thank you,

Jordan Gottlieb
Go Green Fundraising
877-448-9746
Follow us on Twitter
Friend us on Facebook

Yoga

Yoga on the train? Yes! A news report was published in the Montreal Gazette recently saying how many overstressed Germans still hide behind their papers rather than exercise. We're sure Americans and Canadians are no less guilty.

Dear Troy Bonar:

I am a yoga and posture instructor and I run my own yoga studio in Petaluma, CA. It definitely keeps me busy running my business as a "solo-preneur".

What I do to stay fit when busy is to make sure I keep up my yoga practice, even if only for 10-15 minutes in the morning. I also try to ride my bike to work when the weather permits. This may take slightly longer than driving, but saves money and gas, keeps me fit, and is much easier on the environment!

If you want more information about my work, you can visit my website at www.sonomabodybalance.com.

Take care,
Dana Davis

So these commuters are being taught yoga and relaxation techniques on their way to and from work. Instructors are now in what the German government calls "wellness trains" in southern Germany. This was an initiative taken by Deutsche Bahn – Germany's state-owned railway. The organization decided to offer relaxation and yoga techniques to calm an anxious work force.

Discover easy quick yoga poses for beginners and inflexible in a 15 minutes routine at www.synergybyjasmine.com

Stretch.　Play.　Relax.

info@jasminepartneryoga.com
Follow us for inspiring quotes, vitality, meditation & yoga
http://twitter.com/synergyjasmine -
Facebook - http://www.facebook.com/couplesyoga?sk=wall

Online Instant Gift Certificates for Classes for Birthdays, Anniversaries, Holidays, Valentines Day and Weddings.

Synergy By Jasmine!

Section 4   : Exercise Equipment "To Go"

If you're busy but want to integrate exercise into your daily routine, carrying the treadmill around would give you a serious back injury.   We're referring to portable tools that you can take with you to the office, keep in the trunk of your car, or pack into your suitcase:

- ✓ elastic bands
- ✓ light dumb bells
- ✓ jump rope
- ✓ inflatable Swiss balls (the small ones)
- ✓ an exercise video or DVD that you can play in between meetings
- ✓ Yoga mat.
- ✓ Meditation or relaxation music tapes handy.
- ✓ Exercise tubes with handles (to increase muscle strength) and bow tie exerciser (increases upper body strength).

Great product! Field Tested by Troy himself!

www.fitdesk.net

"You definitely want to check the FitDesk™ I can write, watch movies, read, check email, shop online auctions, this is great!"-Troy Bonar

More Portable Exercise Tools!

The choices in other portable exercise tools are impressive:

- ✓ **The Ankle Tough Rehab System** is a set of straps made of heavy-duty elastic, and are cut and stitched to make 2 straps that fit over shoes or bare feet. Set comes with 4 different resistance straps for light, medium, strong and tough resistance levels. Comes also with exercise manual.[11]

---

[11] Hwww.pmtionline.com

✓ **Flex Bars** - a portable exercise gadget that is lightweight. The bars improve grip strength and upper body strength, and allow oscillation movements for neuromuscular and balance training.[12]

✓ **Weighted Vest** – a gadget to help you add resistance to your workout. Vest is weight-adjustable with each weight packet weighing approximately 0.75 lbs, and its one size fits all feature makes it deal for both men and women. Steel shot packets conform to the body, and weight adjustments range from 0.75 lbs. to 20 lbs.[13]

---

[12] Hwww.pmtionline.com

[13] Hwww.target.com

Hello,

I hope this finds you well.

I currently host my own fitness radio talk show called, "Zetlin Fitness" every Saturday at noon on wksc 1300am. You can also listen to it on: www.healthbeatradio.com.

Foremost, with the stresses of everyday life and having little time for ourselves, it's proving very difficult to make the effort to get to the gym. It has been proven that exercise can reduce stress and even eliminate anxiety.

Even with this knowledge, many of us simply don't have energy or are able to create the time management skills needed to work out. However, this should not translate into not exercising.

Enclosed below are some tips that can help balance even the most busiest of schedules to make sure exercise is included.

STABILITY BALL-
Probably one of the most popular pieces of equipment at any gym, however most aren't sure how to train with the ball. For those suffering with only a limited time to exercise, the stability ball can be utilized not only to effectively work the core, but performing any exercise with the ball will result in more calories being burned due to the instability it provides. Depending on your fitness levels, the ball can be used for everything from performing a basic crunch to an advanced push up. Furthermore, other exercises that can be done with the ball include hamstring curls, jackknifes, leg extensions and ball bridges. The stability ball is an excellent way to track your progress and provides limitless exercises to prevent boredom.

DUMBBELLS –
The resistance, range of motion and increased muscle fiber recruitment make the dumbbells the obvious choice over the standard barbell. Efficient exercises that can be performed with dumbbells are presses, rows, laterals and curls. You could even hold them to provide more resistance when doing a squat or lunge. For the more advanced individual, apply the use of dumbbells with the stability ball for a total body workout and an incredible time saver to get the most out of your work out.

FOAM ROLLERS-
 Many of us do not have time to stretch or even neglect a stretching routine, but it is extremely important to have flexibility in your muscles. The foam roller is used to create a deep intense stretch similar to a massage. The foam's hard stable surface helps aid in muscle recovery by creating a powerful release in the stress of your muscular fibers. In other words, it helps improve flexibility by just laying on the area you want to stretch for 30 seconds. You can stretch your hamstrings, calves, quadriceps, hip flexors and different areas of your back all on the foam and be done in no time!

CONSISTENCY-
The key word to any successful workout program is consistency. By keeping consistent workouts, all of my clients have progressed and have continued to set even higher goals for themselves. My clientele have stayed consistent even with their busy work schedule because most crave that structure that their work life already requires of them. I even saw many of them begin to come early before our sessions since they psychologically seemed excited to be back in the gym, and all have started to consider themselves "athletes" no matter what their physical level. This is definitely due to the fact that most busy executives want to feel powerful in any situation.

The gym makes anyone feel strong and especially those that are more advanced than the average person. Power is a strong tool to keep anyone motivated. I hope these tips have been helpful to your readers.

If you find the time, please feel free to visit my website: www.zetlinfitness.com

Thank you very much!

Shaun Zetlin
Master Trainer

HI!

Growing up with a love of food and aversion to exercise, Taisha weighed nearly 300 pounds by age 23. Realizing she needed to make a change, Taisha lost 130 pounds without giving up her appreciation for food. In the process she learned to love exercise and even became a personal trainer! Taisha has maintained her weight loss for over six years and loves to share her secrets with the world. Her philosophy is "It Worked For Me, And it Can Work For You Too!"

Deriving inspiration and information from both Dr. Oz and Oprah, Taisha devotes her life and career to supporting others who are struggling to lose weight. Her website THayesFitness.com is a motivational weight loss resource that details her journey to shed 130 pounds and shares free tips, information, support and inspiration to others struggling with weight issues. Taisha is an AFAA - Aerobics Certified Personal Trainer with THayesFitness & Northwest Sport

Visit www.THayesFitness.comfor My her full 130lb Weight Loss Success story!

Taisha Hayes
THAYESFITNESS
Keeping You Motivated!
www.THayesFitness.com

IMPORTANT NOTE: Buyer Beware!

There are some exercise aids that have been specifically marketed to walkers – things like weighted shoes to add resistance while jogging or brisk-walking. Before you dole out your cash to buy exercise accessories, speak to a fitness trainer or orthopedist first. Some products can be just commercial hype. This article on www.walking.about.com can shed some light on the subject.

If you're going cross-country driving and the trip will take about 12-15 hours, schedule hourly stops so you can perform some stretching exercises, or go for a 15-minute walk in the neighborhood. Exercising will energize you, diminishing your need for frequent cups of coffee and relieve eye strain.

Fitness & Health for the Busy Professional

Awesome Resource!!! Right here!

Hi,
I am a fitness practitioner/personal trainer and designed the IsoBreathing program in early 2003 specifically for the busy professional who can't find the time in their schedules to fit in exercise. What I tell everyone is it is what you have accomplished by the end of the day that counts because not everyone can take an hour to work out.

All you need is two minute increments and that includes an exercise and stretch.

Start first thing in the morning when you are brushing your teeth. Ladies love working inner and outer thighs. With their electric toothbrush in hand they will work outer thigh and stretch. When flossing their teeth they will work inner thigh and stretch. Men prefer full leg such as a wall squat.

When sitting in a carpool line you can work upper body with your steering wheel such as chest, biceps, triceps, and even abdominals. Those exercises just mentioned can also be done while sitting at a desk.

Did you ever think that you could get a full body workout by using your grocery cart while waiting to check out?

My latest book Multitasking: Your Fitness For Life Program has the above and many more. My basic IsoBreathing program can be completed anywhere anytime without equipment.

Ellen Miller
IsoBreathing Inc.

PO Box 803183
Dallas Tx. 75380
www.isobreathing.com
ellen@isobreathing.com

I help individuals become less stressed, healthier, more fit and obtain a better quality of life.
If you can BREATHE and you can SIT IsoBreathing will get you FIT!

Troy's Note: Ellen's book Multitasking: Your Fitness For Life Program has made a huge difference in my busy schedule, it goes through common moments that you wouldn't think about and guides you through the exercises that you can do. I especially like the exercises to do while walking the dog! I drive a lot so the car exercises have made a huge difference on my core and arms.- 5 STARS for Fitness!!! Thanks Ellen!

Hotels

Back to the hotel scene: some nice hotels have spa facilities that you can enjoy while on a business trip. Reward yourself with a facial or a massage **AFTER** a session on the treadmill or 10 laps in the pool. This is a great way to unwind for the evening, and an added bonus for the individual on the go.

The old saying, "You have to enjoy your exercise, otherwise you'll give up in no time" has never been truer.

Here's a tip. If you can't incorporate a tennis game or a trip to the gym, how about signing up for dance classes (e.g. ballet, jazz, tap, belly dancing). If you've always loved dancing as a child, wouldn't this be a great way to fit exercise into a busy schedule?

When you are busy, it is especially important to stay fit. Think of the airplane, if the cabin loses pressure you need oxygen, put the mask on yourself first. You can't take care of others if you are not alive and well yourself. Start your day with a work out. Make it count by doing at least 25 minutes of cardio. Your whole day will go better. Another option is to break up a busy day. Again the time you spend exercising, you will make up with increased efficiency. Also remember you can stretch every hour.

Eva Ritvo, MD
Co author of The Beauty Prescription

If you don't particularly look forward to being with the gym crowd, a dance class will help you stick to the program.

A good motivator – or exercise aid – is to invest in good dance music CD's. Or listen to selected dance tunes on your iPod while traveling, so when you get to your hotel room, you're pumped up and ready to shake that booty!

When it is busy, I tell people to "commercial-cize" -- which means exercise during commercial breaks. In many families, there is a lot of TV time, so why not exercise during the commercials. This idea that has been quite successful for me. Len Saunders - - www.fitkidsbooks.com

DR. LIU'S ULTIMATE LIFESTYLE DIET Sept, 2010—Los Angeles, CA— Bariatric surgeon and weight loss expert Dr. Carson Liu (www.drcarsonliu.com) releases his Ultimate Lifestyle Diet. "Obesity is much about behavior, not just eating the wrong foods," notes Dr. Liu. "Most people view diets as a temporary and time consuming activity." Dr. Liu's Ultimate Lifestyle Diet recommends 10 easy, guilt-free actions that will make a difference for a lifetime. Dr. Liu points out that the best diet technique is to make multiple simple changes in behavior that will help move a person towards a better and healthier life. Dr. Liu's Ultimate Lifestyle Diet

1. Don't eat packaged food that has the word Fructose or a chemical with numbers in the ingredients.

2. Don't eat food that is delivered to your house or through your car window.

3. Before shopping for food eat a meal. Never shop hungry.

4. Switch out sodas for sparkling water, candy for carob chips and high calorie snacks for nuts and fruit.

5. Cook your own meals and reduce the portion size of bread, rice, pasta and potatoes.

6. Eat from small plates.

7. Eat slowly using a child's size spoon, knife or fork.

8. Wait 20 minutes before having a second helping.

9. Don't eat while watching TV.

10. Turn off your computer and or TV for 1 hour per day and take a walk.

"Obesity is at epidemic proportions in the USA" notes Dr. Liu. "The good news is the cure is simple, inexpensive and easily achievable. _Bio: Dr. Carson Liu, Bariatric Surgeon and weight-loss expert, received his medical degree from the University of Chicago, Pritzker School of Medicine and completed his internship, residencies and research fellowship at UCLA Medical Center. Dr. Liu is board certified in General Surgery and over the course of his career has performed over 2600 Bariatric Surgeries. For more information, visit www.drcarsonliu.com _

Using a Pedometer

This is a beeper-sized device that you clip to your waistband. It measures walking and running distance in steps and miles. Some models are more sophisticated and equipped with measuring features for pace, total exercise time and calories burned.

Troy's Tip: "You should try to add 1,000 extra steps to your day."

A pedometer could motivate you to walk during airport or train layovers because you'll know how much ground you've covered and will encourage you to aim for a longer distance on your next trip. Joe Decker says he tested 6 models for accuracy and 4 out of the 6 were accurate. He recommends two specifically: Bodytronics Q25 Electronic Pedometer and the Part Ultrak 275 Electronic Calorie Pedometer.[14]

---

[14] Joe Decker.

Hi Troy,
My name is Stephanie, and I am a fun Health & Fitness Expert. I do TV segments and train private clients on how to incorporate fitness into their everyday lives. I created the Cubicle Crunch:
http://www.stepitupwithsteph.com/tag/cubicle_crunch/ and other things to do around the house, at work, and after work to make time for even a 5 minute run, 50 crunches, and other things to do for your body.

I believe that all of this comes with a shift in your MINDSET - being active doesnt need to involve an hour at the gym.

Being active and fit is a mindset and once working out is not viewed as a burden or a chore, it is seen as something fun to do and a happy part of a busy day.

To the life that YOU want,
Stephanie Mansour CEO
Step It Up with Steph
Health & Fitness Expert
Body Image & Confidence Coach

Quick, free workouts: Turbo Abs, Butts, Yoga, & more!
www.StepItUpwithSteph.com

LOSE WEIGHT EVEN IF YOU'RE BUSY

And who isn't busy? We've been talking about how fast-paced and hectic our lifestyles are. The idea of losing weight typically generates rather glamorous images: personal trainers, hours in the gym on complicated equipment, expensive groceries and making a veritable career out of cooking dinner.

Statistically, WE'RE BOTH THE BUSIEST AND FATTEST BUNCH OF PEOPLE ON EARTH, so it's not hard to see why the thought of weight loss carries such impossibly glamorous, time-sucking connotations. Fortunately, our idea of what's required is not really accurate – whether you want to lose ten pounds or fifty. Of course, diet pills and exercise gadgets you see on infomercials don't work – it's not quite _that_ easy. But losing weight is surprisingly simple if you apply a few tips consistently.

HERE ARE TEN OF MY FAVORITE WAYS TO GET STARTED TODAY:

10. NO MORE FRIVOLOUS BREAD

What's the harm of one roll at dinner, right? A lot more than you think. Bread baskets are ubiquitous, and they're also worthless. Make it a habit to avoid these freebie wasteful calories, period. After a few weeks you will notice a difference. It's too easy!

9. DON'T EAT UNTIL YOU'RE STUFFED

This seems obvious, but many of us are guilty of over-eating. I was surprised to learn recently that liver disease is an alarming new problem (truly an epidemic), but _not_ because of excessive alcohol consumption.

It's because of excessive food consumption! It's really true that restaurant portions are two to three times more than you need – and that's standard. Here's how to deal: eat until that point where your stomach is no longer growling, but you could still eat a bit more. From now on, simply stop when you get to that point. It only takes one or two times to realize how incredible this feels. The busiest person can eat less.

8. GET IT TO GO

I'm not talking about take-out. Anytime you dine out, get half the meal into a doggy bag before you even start. You don't have to cook all your meals to lose weight; just eat less when you are out. Hey, you'll save cash, too!

7. DON'T DRINK CALORIES

Many of us consume several hundred empty, sugary calories daily without realizing it – lattes, sodas, "energy" drinks, sports drinks, smoothies and so on. Unless these drinks are replacing a meal or supplementing a really small meal, don't drink them. I like to have frequent protein and fiber smoothies, but they typically replace a meal, or I make sure to get in a really intense workout session.

What to do: stick with water and the occasional glass of wine or a light beer. Make calorie-rich drinks a treat, because they really are more like dessert and should be viewed as such. That daily latte is packing on as much as half a pound a week. It's easy to see why people can gain ten or fifteen pounds a year without knowing why – these little treats have a terrible cumulative affect on your waistline (and health). Busy and need a lift? Grab a water bottle to go instead of a mocha. Realize that most of these drinks are really just glorified milkshakes.

6. REALIZE WHY YOU NEED TO LOSE WEIGHT

Most of us get caught up in the vanity of weight loss – we just want to look good! There's nothing wrong with that. But remember that being overweight is behind most of the major causes of death in this country – and nearly all of them are preventable! This isn't about having the perfect abs or being a size 4. Even a ten-pound weight loss can add years of good health to your life. Time it takes to realize this: you just did!

5. Snack, Part A

We have become a culture of constant eaters. We're always snacking – bars, chips, bags of treats, candy, cheese, it never ends. We often eat more than the serving size when we snack (who ever eats only seven chips?). Learn to slow down and enjoy meals, and think about the calories you're putting into your mouth. Simply practice being aware of everything you eat. This doesn't take up your time, and it makes a big difference in how much you eat.

4. SNACK, PART B

When you snack, snack on fruit or veggies. Your body will soon grow to crave them instead of the other unhealthy treats. Humans become easily habituated to any substance – make this work for you, not against you. Busy folks have no excuse: pre-washed, chopped veggies are available in most grocery stores, and you can always get the kids to take on the chore of tossing rinsed veggies into baggies for a week's worth of snacks all ready to grab and go.

3. LUNCH DILEMMAS

Many of us eat too much or chow on unhealthy lunches because we're in a rush or just can't get away from the desk. Two easy, quick fixes for even the busiest souls:

- If you eat home-made lunches, you don't have to keep buying and consuming the same old pre-made junk. Buy and consume bagged salads instead. There is almost always one variety of bagged lettuce on sale. Keep a bottle of balsamic vinegar at work, and you're good to go. This doesn't take any more time than microwaving a pre-made meal high in carbohydrates and bad fats and you'll save thousands of calories (translation: a couple of pounds) a week.

- If you and the gang dine out for lunch, just start ordering salads instead of sandwiches and pastas. Lay off the croutons and franken-dressings, and you're well on your way to losing weight in just a few weeks. Salads shouldn't be a once-in-a-while healthy notion. Greens of some sort should be a daily habit. They are what we are meant to eat.

2. FROZEN VEGETABLES ARE YOUR FRIENDS

Too tired to whip up a healthy, nutritious dinner? We all are. Fortunately, healthy dinners really don't take very long. In fact, heating up a huge bag of vegetables and drenching them in olive oil and tasty spices takes less time than waiting for the pizza to arrive. Get into the habit of eating veggies for dinner at least 3 or 4 days a week, and watch the pounds RUN. IN. TERROR.

I eat pretty light dinners, but if you need more protein in your evening meal, bake up a big bag of frozen chicken breasts once a week so they're ready to slice and toss into the vegetables. Now seriously, did that take any time at all?

1. BOTTOM LINE

For people on the go, the bottom line for weight loss comes down to reducing portions. AVOID THE EMPTY CALORIE TRAPS – PRE-MADE MEALS, COFFEE DRINKS, SNACKS. These are the bane of any busy person's existence. Avoiding them doesn't mean you must alternatively slave over freshly-made meals or spend hours at the gym every week.

And recognize that convenience and speed apply equally to vegetables and low-calorie foods like salads, too. So make the better choice.

http://www.marksdailyapple.com

Mark Sisson is the author of five books on exercise and nutrition and is founder and CEO of Primal Nutrition, Inc., and of MarksDailyApple.com, a top-ranked health and fitness blog with more than 30,000 vistors a day. A former world-class endurance athlete (2:18 marathon, 4th place Hawaii Ironman), Sisson also served as Anti-doping Commissioner of International Triathlon Union and its liaison to the IOC. At __an early age, Sisson was forced to retire from athletic competition due to IBS, chronic upper respiratory infections, tendonitis, and osteoarthritis that arose from his so-called "healthy" lifestyle. Using his pre-medical background (B.A. degree in biology, Williams College), athletic experience, 25 years of research, Sisson developed a revolutionary diet and fitness regimen that turned around his health. Today at 57 Sisson is healthier and fitter than when he raced marathons and triathlons and devotes his research and experience to helping others reprogram their genes the primal way.

Always Carry...

Always have the following items with you as you travel:

- comfortable shoes
- padlock
- foldable, light gym bag
- quick dry clothing

Keep these in your suitcase at all times so you don't waste time looking for them and re-packing them. A busy individual like you need not be unencumbered by exercise paraphernalia that you're hunting for just before taking a flight!

When our schedules become crazy busy the first thing that goes is exercise. The best way to make it happen is to schedule it on your calendar and it will be more likely it happen. **Or** work-out first thing in the morning, that way you don't have time to think of excuses not to do it. By the time you are in the shower, you are feeling great and you can cross one more thing off of your list. You win.

To ensure you and your family are eating healthy, be prepared. After you go to the grocery store allow for an hour or so to prep your foods for the week. By doing this you will not be throwing out food that has become penicillin. For example, when you cut up your celery and place it on the shelf of the fridge, you are more likely to eat it. If it stays in stalk all wrapped up and hidden away in a drawer, the probability of you eating it is slim to none. Take your fruits and veggies out of the drawers and put them in containers on the shelves so when you open your fridge, they are the first thing you see.

Judy Weitzman
Diet Coach Judy LLC
f/d/a Motivation Plus LLC
500 N Michigan Avenue - Suite 300
Chicago, IL 60611
312.560.2900
Fax 866.854.5734
www.dietcoachjudy.com

Keep a Record!

A workout log would be nice – just to monitor your progress. When you become pleased with yourself, liking yourself for the small efforts you've invested into improving your physical self, you may want to get into a full-fledged workout program with a trainer.

Show him/her your workout log so he knows exactly how fit you are.

Eating Fit!

Let's not forget your fuel! Don't run low on gas; otherwise your body cannot achieve optimum fitness performance.

Busy professionals need healthy snacks. Forget the protein bars, the quality ones taste like cardboard and the tasty ones spike your insulin. I developed a tasty, nutritious, and inexpensive snack recipe called THE HEALING TRAIL MIX to complement my fantastic new book called WHOLE HEALTH HEALING - THE BUDGET FRIENDLY NATURAL WELLNESS BIBLE FOR ALL AGES.

* The Healing Trail Mix
- 1 cup raisins
- 1 cup unsalted walnuts
- 1 cup roasted, shelled unsalted pumpkin seeds
- 1 cup unsalted roasted soy nuts
-1 cup carob chips
 - 1 /4 teaspoon sea salt.

Why is it healing? Healing demands specific nutrients like these for cellular rebuilding, balanced body chemistry and optimum organ function. For example: The raisins and carob are high in fiber and anti-oxidants, known to reduce cancer risk. The walnuts contain essential oils like Omega 3 known to reduce the risk of cardiovascular disease and enhance brain function.

The pumpkin seeds contain nutrients known to aid men's prostates The soy nuts are known to help balance women's hormones. The sea salt is a healthier alternative than conventional salt because sea salt contains many minerals. This recipe is overall a tasty balance of protein/carbs/healthy fats/fiber, and has a low glycemic index (does not spike insulin).

-Dr Potisk is known as the "Down-to-Earth" doctor http://www.thedowntoearthdoctor.com because of his holistic lifestyle and practical, good-natured teaching ability.

-AUTHOR OF:
WHOLE HEALTH HEALING : THE BUDGET FRIENDLY NATURAL WELLNESS BIBLE FOR ALL AGES
(http://www.wholehealthhealing.com)
Author of the book specifically for doctors:
RECLAIM THE JOY OF PRACTICE: AN ADVANCED GUIDE FOR ADVANCING DOCTORS
(http://www.reclaimthejoy.com) –

Dr. Tom Potisk the "Down-to-Earth" doctor.

Doctor of Chiropractic since 1984 -Chiropractor of the Year award winner -additional certifications in nutritional counseling and wellness -hosted live call-in radio show To Your Health for 2 years -father of 3 children ages 10,12,14. God help me!

Popular blog/web sites for the general public:
http://www.thedowntoearthdoctor.com,
http://www.wholehealthhealing.com
Specifically for doctors: http://www.reclaimthejoy.com

Nuts, sesame snacks, protein bars, low-fat muffins, a generous helping of dried and fresh fruit, baby carrots, cereal flakes, oatmeal bars should keep you on the go while exercising.

If you're pressed for time to sit down for a proper meal, these portable foods will tide you over, in a healthy and nutritious way.

Fitness & Health for the Busy Professional

Hi,

For me, the big challenge is cooking healthy meals. You can exercise all you want; but if you're not eating healthy, your body will not be healthy either.

 Through my own struggles in the kitchen, I created the book "I'd Rather Scrub Toilets Than Cook!" It provides tips to getting in and out of the kitchen quickly, plus over fifty simple, easy, delicious and healthy recipes.

Here are three tips from my book that can help you create healthy meals at home:

1. Keep a stock of staple foods, plus fresh fruits and vegetables, so you always have something available.

 2. Cut up foods you use frequently (like onions and peppers) all at once. Doing this allows you to "grab a handful" and prepare quickly, versus having to cut every time you cook.

 3. Cook once, eat thrice. Cooking more than you need allows you to re-use food later in the week, making preparation time shorter.

Warm Regards,

Gina Van Luven, H.C.

Health and Nutrition Counselor

YOUnique NutritionÂ® Wellness solutions to support your mind, body and soul.
gvanluven@youniquenutrition.com

www.YOUniqueNutrition.com

THE GREEN NUT

A BUSY SCHEDULE DOESN'T HAVE TO MEAN ABANDONING YOUR HEALTHY EATING HABITS WHILE ON THE GO. CHOOSING A SNACK THAT'S NOT ONLY EASY TO TAKE ALONG BUT IS ALSO FULL OF NUTRIENTS TO KEEP YOU GOING IS THE BEST WAY TO KEEP ENERGIZED THROUGHOUT A HECTIC DAY AT THE OFFICE.

THAT'S WHY PISTACHIOS ARE THE PERFECT SNACK! PISTACHIOS - THE ONLY GREEN NUT - PROVIDE 3G OF FIBER AND 6G OF PROTEIN IN ONE OUNCE, AND ARE A GOOD SOURCE OF AT LEAST FIVE NUTRIENTS, SUCH AS COPPER AND THIAMIN.

ONE SERVING IS A WHOPPING 49 NUTS - MORE THAN ANY OTHER TREE NUT - AND PROVIDES ONLY 2G OF SUGAR IN 160 CALORIES! NOT ONLY WILL PISTACHIOS HELP KEEP YOUR HUNGER AT BAY, & THEY MAY ACTUALLY REDUCE YOUR BODY'S RESPONSE TO STRESS. A STUDY DONE BY PENN STATE(HTTP://WWW.THEGREENNUT.ORG/PISTACHIO HEALTH/RESEARCH/24) FOUND THAT EATING A DAILY DOSE OF PISTACHIOS, ALONG WITH A HEALTHY DIET AND EXERCISE, CAN LESSEN THE BIOLOGICAL REACTIONS TO STRESS.

TRY INCORPORATING PISTACHIOS INTO YOUR DIET BEFORE, DURING AND AFTER A CHAOTIC MONDAY, THAT BIG MEETING OR STRESSFUL EVENTS THAT MIGHT WEAR YOU DOWN THROUGHOUT THE WEEK.

TO KEEP YOURSELF FULL AND ENERGIZED WITHOUT THROWING OFF YOUR DIET, TRY SOME OF THESE HEALTHY SNACKING TIPS:

* SNACK AND HYDRATE! TO AVOID OVEREATING, NEVER LET YOURSELF GET FAMISHED. TRY KEEPING A HANDY PACK OF PISTACHIOS WITH YOU AT ALL TIMES IN CASE HUNGER HITS UNEXPECTEDLY. AND MAKE SURE TO DRINK PLENTY OF WATER -- WHEN YOU ARE DEHYDRATED YOU FEEL HUNGRIER.

* KEEP A DISH OF PISTACHIOS WITHIN REACH AT YOUR WORKSPACE FOR WHEN THAT AFTERNOON HUNGER STRIKES.

* IF YOU'RE LOOKING TO LOWER YOUR SNACK CALORIES, THINK ABOUT REACHING FOR THE GREEN NUT. CRACKING OPEN THE SHELL CONSEQUENTIALLY SLOWS DOWN YOUR SNACKING, THUS CAUSING YOU TO NATURALLY CONSUME LESS CALORIES. PLUS, THERE ARE 49 PISTACHIOS PER SERVING, MORE THAN ANY OTHER SNACK NUT.

* MIX PISTACHIOS INTO YOUR ORDINARY RECIPES FOR SOME ADDED NUTRITION. PISTACHIOS CONTAIN OVER 30 NECESSARY VITAMINS AND MINERALS, SO TRY ADDING THEM TO MUFFINS OR GRANOLA FOR AN EXTRA BOOST OF ENERGY.

* ADDED BONUS: PISTACHIOS, WHEN EATEN WITH SOME HIGH-CARBOHYDRATE FOODS, MAY HELP CURB BLOOD SUGAR SPIKES - AN IMPORTANT FACTOR IN PREVENTING DIABETES.

* KEEP A SUPPLY OF BROWN RICE, FROZEN VEGGIES AND PISTACHIOS IN YOUR KITCHEN. IF YOU\'RE IN A MAJOR TIME CRUNCH, YOU CAN THROW THESE ITEMS TOGETHER WITH A BIT OF

LOW-SODIUM SOY SAUCE AND SEASONINGS FOR A
QUICK AND TASTY STIR-FRY MEAL.

* PISTACHIOS ARE A GREAT PROTEIN SUBSTITUTE.
IF YOU DON'T HAVE TIME TO GO GROCERY
SHOPPING EVERY WEEK, KEEP SOME PISTACHIOS
ON HAND FOR WHEN YOU RUN OUT OF FRESH MEAT,
POULTRY OR FISH.

FOR HEALTHY RECIPES AND MORE TIPS ON
INCORPORATING PISTACHIOS INTO YOUR DIET,
VISIT WWW.THEGREENNUT.ORG.

-VICTORIA GESTNER

Howdy Troy!
A great fitness tip for busy professionals is to take the stairs
when you can. Get off the bus or subway a stop early to get
some walking in.

Take a break from your desk at least once a day and walk
around the block.

Instead of buzzing your co-worker to ask a question walk
over. It only takes a minute and you will get the benefit of
moving around. My guess is your co-worker will appreciate it
as well.

Tips for health: Leave healthy snacks at your desk. We are
so busy we often don't get proper nutrition.

If you cant take a break for lunch or find yourself skipping
meals make sure you have snacks at your desk you can
munch on throughout the day. A bowl of cherry tomatoes
are great to munch on. Nuts give us tons of energy. Lara

bars are made from whole ingredients like nuts and fruit and come in tons of flavours that taste great and can be a great quick energy packed punch when needed.

Leave a huge glass of water on your desk. Staying hydrated is so important for our bodies. it helps our minds stay sharp. Replacing your designer water drink or fancy coffee drink can not only cut down on extra calories and sugar but can keep you from the energy roller coaster that sugars give us.

Robin Fischman, HHC, AADP
Health Coach
www.robinfischman.com
(917) 930-4072
Connect with me on Facebook:

"Eat food. Not too much. Mostly plants." - Michael Pollan

5

Section 5: Information/Resources for the Hurried and Harried

The One-Minute Exercises Book of Denise Austin contains quick exercises. While quick food is junk food, quick exercise is not junk exercise and therefore must be scoffed at. If you can afford to squeeze in only five minutes at certain times of the day, this book is a boon.

Not only does it contain one-minute exercises, it takes into account that you'd want to increase your workout duration eventually, so it includes 5-minute and 10-minute exercises.

The book was published more than 10 years ago, but you still see Denise Austin featured on www.msn.com, so she must tap into some of her older exercise programs. Workout programs never get outmoded or go stale.

Dear Reader:

Alicia Rockmore and Sarah Welch are the co-founders of Buttoned Up, inc - a company dedicated to helping busy people get organized sanely. Both women juggle full personal (taking care of young children and aging parents) and professional lives. Yet these two co-authors, businesswomen, 'mompreneurs' find - no they MAKE - the time to work out and keep healthy. Below are some of the organizational tricks they use (and frequently recommend to others) to actually take care of their own health in spite of very full to-do lists.

ORGANIZING FOR WEIGHT LOSS TIPS

#1. Keep Track Of Your Progress

As much as we wish it were true, transformation doesn't happen just by getting that gym membership. You need to set goals, plan how to reach them, and keep track of your progress. We use a cool thing called Fitness.doc, available at www.getbuttonedup.com to help stay focused and on track. It's got three sections: one for setting goals, one for food, and weight tracking, and one for tracking your exercise progress.

#2 Find and Exercise Buddy

It's a lot harder to drop off your routine if you've got another person doing it with you. The added motivation of one more person helps keep you on track, plus you've got someone with whom you can be secretly (or not so secretly) competitive to see who is getting in better shape. When you add a partner to the mix, those New Year's Resolutions quickly change from a chore, to something you actually look forward to.

#3 Once a Week Peace of Mind

When you work up a good sweat, you often find peace of mind. But when you're juggling many different responsibilities it can be difficult to get in a decent, hour-long workout (plus time for shower/change). Rather than beat yourself up for failing to carve out an additional 60 minutes in your day, embrace your reality. Walk briskly at lunch at least 3 days a week as your regular cardio. Then, once, on the weekend - best option is first thing Saturday morning I - take a full hour to work out. If you have children, you see if you can alternate watching the kids one weekend morning with your spouse so that each of you gets one day to recharge with a proper workout.

#4 Expect Imperfection

One thing you can count on if you're dieting is that you will have a weak moment. All too often, people feel that if they succumb to the siren call of a cookie (or three) that they have failed and they might as well give up. That's just plain crazy. Don't let a moment or two of weakness derail your overall effort. Instead, have one or two things that you can do _immediately_ after a weak moment to get yourself back on track. You might want to take a brisk ten minute walk, call a diet buddy who can talk you off the ledge.

#5 Make "I Will" Resolutions/Goals vs. "I Won't"

Try a new twist on the whole resolution thing. Instead of coming up with a list of "I won't" statements I have decided to compile a list of "I will" ones. Psychologically, wording a resolution can make a world of difference in how we respond in our behaviors. For example, instead of 'I won't eat junk food' try 'I will treat myself to one sweet snack every other day,' or instead of 'I won't ever skip a weekday workout' try 'I will do something active for at least thirty minutes Monday-Friday.'

ORGANIZING FOR HEALTHY EATING TIPS

#1: PREP HEALTHY SNACKS IN ADVANCE: on Sunday night after all the little ones are in bed asleep, grab a few carrots, a cucumber, and an apple. Chop them up into snack-sized pieces and put them into Ziploc bags so anyone can grab a healthy nibble during the week. It takes 5 minutes - 7 max!

#2: WHEN IT COMES TO MEAL PLANNING, DELEGATE, DELEGATE, DELEGATE: The number one reason people turn to less than healthy take out or pre-prepped grocery meals is fatigue and lack of planning. But when your schedule is overflowing, finding the time to plan is easier said than done. The good news - take some of the burden for planning off of your plate! - Keep a running shopping list on a notepad in the kitchen that anyone can take to the store to buy the groceries at any point during the week. If you have staples you always need to buy, - Have kids over 3 but under 10 set the table and kids over 10 help prep the meal. - On Sunday afternoon, have each member of the family pick the menu for one night of the week. That's a few less meals for you to figure out AND you'll know at least one other person will like what's for dinner that night! - Institute the rule: if you cooked it, you're off the hook for cleaning up and doing the dishes.

#3: PREP STAPLES IN ADVANCE: if you use vegetables like onions, carrots and broccoli in a lot of different meals, pre-prep them all at once when you have time. Keep them fresh in Ziploc bags in the fridge so they're ready to go when you need them in a flash during the week. This can cut 10-20 minutes from your nightly meal routine! If you're using browned meat or grilled chicken in a few recipes during the week - brown it/grill it when you get it home from the store and put it in the fridge so all you have to do during the week is reheat. * GO GREEN: you can make pretty incredible salads in about 10 minutes. Just go to the fridge, take out all the veggies you have, find a protein, cut it all up and throw it together in a bowl. Voila - you've got a delicious, hearty meal. If you think kids/husbands won't eat it - you're underestimating the power of ranch dressing (or the game of choosing the best salad dressing).

Take a sec and sign up for our e-newsletter:
http://www.getbuttonedup.com/email-signup/

They're effective today as they were a decade ago. The book is published by Vintage Books (Random House) and the ISBN number is 0-394-74633-3. Researcher and fitness expert Suzanne Schlosberg, who wrote a fitness manual for individuals on the go, did a survey of hotels and airports where the busy traveler can do an abbreviated or full blown workout while they're traveling and waiting for their connecting flights. Here is some information from her work (her book is highly recommended!).

As a test manager for a company that operates around-the-clock, I sometimes need to get creative in order to stay on my balanced eating and fitness program. The one area that requires the most planning is meals.

In my fitness guides "Journey to Fitness" and "Balanced Eating Made Easy", I explain why eating many small meals throughout the day is the key to weight control and maintaining a balanced diet. However, to have all these meals prepared ahead of time requires planning, as your worst enemy is procrastination – waiting until you are hungry to decide what to eat.

With a couple of meals packed the night before, I reserve any reading duties, such as correspondence or reviewing documents, for times in the morning and afternoon where I can leisurely eat while working. This leaves my so-called "lunch break" free for a brisk walk, or a swim at a local pool. Any time spent over my allotted one hour is made up by staying a little later that same day.

On days when it is just not possible to leave work in the middle of the day, I make sure to reserve thirty minutes to an hour for exercise after work. To avoid the drive time and crowds of my health club, I have a few of my favorite pieces of exercise equipment at home to alternate between, including a treadmill, exercise bike, weights, and a stability ball.

The most important thing to remember when planning your own fitness program is that staying fit needs to be a part of your daily lifestyle, and not an afterthought to fit into your busy schedule.

Best always,
Art Dragon

Hello!

I am the founder and eco-entrepreneur of an organic gardening company. I am also a single mom with 2 children aged 8 and 10, 2 dogs and a home and garden. Whew, right? Building a successful company based on living a green and healthy lifestyle with distributors throughout the US and Canada means that I have to represent my company as a woman living a green and healthy lifestyle too. How do I do this? As a vegetarian, I eat only foods that are low glycemic so that I experience a sustained energy level throughout the day ensuring I am most productive during work hours. I make sure I get a minimum of 7.5 hours of sleep a night and I exercise on a daily basis. I have to split my excerise into (2) mini-sessions a day. I do 20 minutes of cardio in the morning before getting the kids up for school. I then do a 30-40 minute workout in the evening balancing cardio, strength and toning. I also meditate 2-3 times a week and work in the garden for spiritual restoration. I will be 41 this month and look and feel better than I have ever! I have been a single mom for the past 3 years so I have had to make major adjustments to my routine and daily diet to make sure no one is neglected, including myself :-)

Happy Gardening!
Annette Pelliccio
Founder & CEO
The Happy Gardener, Inc
www.thehappygardener.info

Want to know more about The Happy Gardener and our eco-efforts?
Listen in on our 5-minute recording at 616-712-8099 with access code 746208#

Troy's Tip:

Another Great book for your personal and professional life is Darren Hardy's Book THE COMPOUND EFFECT. It talks about how to track your success and also how the small changes you make will change your life. www.thecompoundeffect.com

Troy's FAT Bank Book Plug #2:

I have a special book for people who do not or can not exercise very well and still want to lose weight, THE FAT BANK. It talks about how to lose hundreds of pounds without adding exercise until you are ready and able.

Hi ,

My name is Jill Coleman, ACSM-certified personal trainer, Fitness Coordinator at Wake Forest University and co-author of the My Gym Trainer book series (www.MyTrainerFitness.com).

Finding the time to exercise and eat right is a huge obstacle for many people, and usually the #1 reason they cannot get and stay healthy. Here are some tips that I hope can help you regarding how to eat clean all week with easy, on-the-go meals.

TIPS FOR EATING RIGHT WITH A HECTIC SCHEDULE:

One of the best ways to ensure you have the tools to eat well during the week is to plan and prep for the upcoming week on Sundays.

Food shop, prepare, cook and package meals for easy on-the-go eating during the week. Few people have the time or patience to cook gourmet meals every night for themselves and their families, so having something healthy and READY is key to staying on track with your nutrition. Even the most disciplined will give into the chips and cookies in the cupboard when arriving home after a long day. Sometimes it is easy to eat so much while waiting for dinner to cook that you're not even hungry by the time it's ready! Everyone has been there, so here are some tried and true tricks to healthy meal prep for ready-to-eat convenience.

FOOD SHOPPING

Creating a list ahead of time will help keep things quick, and also keep you on track at the grocery store so you don't end up wandering the aisles aimlessly, picking up Oreos and Doritos.

Here is a great list to get you started:

Ground bison or ground turkey
Eggs/egg whites
Chicken breasts
Spinach
Asparagus
Broccoli
Bell peppers
Sweet potatoes
Grapefruits
Apples
Frozen berries
Oat bran
Unsweetened almond milk
Almond cheese
Unsweetened cocoa powder

Fitness-Friendly Hotels

Suzanne Schlosberg performed some helpful due diligence to help the busy traveler by providing the names of major hotels with gym facilities (US only). An extract from that list:

- ✓ Four Seasons – 95% of their hotels have pools. All of their fitness centers have cardio and weight machines;

- ✓ Ritz Carlton – 80% of their hotels have pools

- ✓ Sheraton Hotels and Resorts – pool facility in 95% of their hotels
- ✓ Westin Hotels and Resorts – all of their hotels have pools.[15]

---

[15] Suzanne Schlosberg

In addition to being a busy business owner myself, I also help busy people balance health goals with hectic lives via my health counseling practice Dalch Wellness (http://dalchwellness.com).

Here's what I've always done to make fitness and healthy eating a priority in my life:

* CHOOSE WORKOUT ROUTINES THAT CAN BE DONE ANYWHERE. I run and do Pilates (which I often do on the floor of a hotel room when I'm traveling). Power walking and yoga are other good options that don't require lots of special equipment (that's the key).

* KEEP QUICK, HEALTHY FOOD ON HAND IN THE KITCHEN. I always have canned beans (with no salt added!), frozen veggies/fruit, and a variety of grains around, just in case I can't make it to the market that day to get fresh veggies, etc.

* WHEN YOU COOK, MAKE ENOUGH FOOD FOR 2 - 3 MEALS. Leftovers can be used the next day for lunch or dinner and can sometimes be stretched into a third day.

* ALWAYS CARRY HEALTHY SNACKS. I like nuts mixed with dried fruit, low-sugar granola bars, or fresh fruit (apples and bananas travel well).

* ALWAYS CARRY A BOTTLE OF WATER. And keep a glass of water by the bed to drink right after you wake up each morning.

* CHOSE 2 - 3 RECIPES TO LEARN AND BE ABLE TO MAKE ON A MOMENT\'S NOTICE. A little time investment upfront, but saves times and stress once you become a pro at those dishes. (I'm happy to share some of my favorite healthy recipe sources/cookbooks if that's of interest.)

-Lara Dalch, Health Counselor at Dalch Wellness (www.dalchwellness.com)

Dalch MarketingBlog | Twitter | Facebook | LinkedIn
Become a Fan of Dalch Wellness on Facebook!

Fitness-Friendly Airports

Schlossberg does not stop with hotel lists!

She also provides a list of airports with massage facilities – you must have seen those massage chairs in strategic locations of large, international airports: Here's a sampling:

- ✓ Chicago: O'Hare International Airport – *A Massage Inc*, level 6, main terminal west (near post office); open 7:30 am to 9:30 pm

- ✓ Boston: Logan International Airport – *A Relaxed Attitude* – terminal B, American Airlines Side, upper level (hours vary);

- ✓ Seattle: Seattle-Tacoma International Airport – *Massage Bar Inc* – Concourse C, beyond security checkpoint, Gates N-16 and N-1

As for fitness centers in airports and near airports, pages 36-38 of Schlosberg's book, *The Ultimate Workout Guide for the Road* (ISBN number 0-618-11592-7) contains a detailed listing of these fitness centers – to help you do your workout on your next airport layover.[16]

Plus workout programs that Schlosberg labels "The Time to Kill Workout", "The Timesaver Workout", "The Bare-Minimum Workout" all designed for the busybody!

---

[16] Suzanne Schlosberg.

GREETINGS,

I AM WRITING ON BEHALF OF THE OAKS AT OJAI, A CALIFORNIA DESTINATION SPA RESORT AND MEMBER OF THE DESTINATION SPA GROUPWITH SOME FIT TIPS FOR BUSY PEOPLE! THE FOUNDER OF OUR SPA IS QUITE THE INSPIRATION PARTICULARLY HOW SHE'S MANAGED TO INCORPORATE FITNESS INTO HER VERY BUSY LIFE! I'VE INCLUDED A RECENT LIST OF TIPS BELOW, BUT ALSO ENCOURAGE YOU TO CHECK FOR MORE OF HER POCKET-SIZED TIPS AT: HTTP://WWW.OAKSSPA.COM/OAKS-SHARES

LOOK 6 YEARS YOUNGER BY TONIGHT-
  BY SHEILA CLUFF
  FOUNDER
  THE OAKS AT OJAI

WHAT IF YOU KNEW YOU COULD LOOK SIX YEARS YOUNGER BY THIS EVENING AND IT WOULD COST LESS THAN $20? YES, THAT'S THE DEAL. WHETHER YOU'RE GOING TO A WORK PARTY, A CLASS REUNION, OR MEETING SOMEONE, ANYONE, YOU WANT TO IMPRESS, WHY SETTLE FOR LESS? HERE ARE SOME TRICKS GATHERED BY MY STAFF AND THOSE IN THE HEALTH, BEAUTY AND FASHION INDUSTRIES.

  *DRINK A TALL GLASS OF WATER EVERY TWO HOURS FOR THE NEXT SIX HOURS. YOU'LL INCREASE THE WATER IN YOUR BODY, WHICH WILL MAKE YOUR SKIN LOOK YOUNGER. YOU'LL ALSO FEEL BETTER SINCE THE MUSCLES AND JOINTS OF YOUR BODY REQUIRE WATER TO MOVE LIKE A YOUNGER PERSON.

  *MOISTURIZE. AFTER A WARM (NOT HOT) SHOWER OR BATH, MOISTURIZE YOURSELF FROM HEAD TO TOE. ALLOW THE MOISTURIZER TO PENETRATE THE OUTERMOST LAYER OF SKIN AND BLOT OF EXCESS.

ON YOUR HEELS, ELBOWS AND FINGER TIPS, MASSAGE IN EXTRA LOTION, OR EVEN HEAVIER OIL, LIKE ALMOND OIL. AGAIN BLOT EXCESS; APPLY MORE LATER IF YOU WANT. MOST WOMEN PREFER MOISTURIZERS THAT HAVE NO SCENT OR MATCH THE SCENT OF THEIR PERFUMES.

*LOOK ONLINE OR WINDOW SHOP AT A DEPARTMENT STORE TO SEE THE CLOTHING STYLES THAT ARE WORN BY PEOPLE YEARS YOUNGER THAN YOU. YOU MIGHT NOT HAVE THE MIDDLE SECTION TO EXPOSE, BUT COULD FIND THAT SHORT OR LONG JACKETS, SKINNY OR FLARED LEG JEANS ARE FLATTERING AND THAT YOU NEED MORE COLOR. TRY ON A FEW DARING OUTFITS TO GET THE FEEL OF HOW IT FEELS TO BE YOUNGER. THEN RETURN HOME AND CHECK OUT YOUR WARDROBE TO SEE WHAT ITEMS YOU CAN PUT TOGETHER IN NEW AND YOUTHFUL WAYS.

*STAND IN FRONT OF A MIRROR AND SLOUCH. NOW, CORRECT YOUR POSTURE. TOUCH THE PART OF YOUR CHEST ABOUT THREE INCHES ABOVE THE NAVEL. NOW PULL YOUR CHEST UP, BUT LOWER YOUR SHOULDERS AND CHECK YOUR IMAGE IN THE MIRROR. YOU ALREADY LOOK MUCH YOUNGER BECAUSE ERECT POSTURE IS A YOUTHFUL ATTRIBUTE.

*PULL IN YOUR TUMMY MUSCLES AND TUCK YOUR BUTT. (PRACTICE STANDING THIS WAY) YOUNGER FOLKS HAVE TIGHT MIDDLE MUSCLES AND YOU CAN TOO.

*CHECK HOW YOU WALK. DO YOU LIFT YOUR FEET OR MOVE LIKE YOU HAVE NO WHERE TO GO? YOUNG PEOPLE ALWAYS SEEM TO BE IN A HURRY. TRY THIS. WALK AROUND THE BLOCK OR YOUR OFFICE BUILDING AS IF YOU'RE VERY LATE FOR AN APPOINTMENT. TUCK YOUR TUMMY AND CORRECT YOUR POSTURE AT THE SAME TIME.

*CHANGE YOUR HAIR. SWEEP IT FORWARD, PART IT ON THE OTHER SIZE, TIE A SCARF AROUND IT. DO

SOMETHING YOU'VE BEEN DREAMING OF, INCLUDING GETTING HOOKED ON HATS. IF YOU WANT TO GO OVER YOUR BUDGET, TALK WITH YOUR HAIR DRESSER ABOUT ADDING HIGHLIGHTS OR BRIGHTENING THE COLOR OF YOUR HAIR. AS WE AGE, SOMETIMES OUR FACIAL COLORS BECOME DULL AND HAIR STREAKED WITH GRAY CAN MAKE US FEEL AND LOOK DRAB.

 *CHECK YOUR MAKE UP. WHEN WAS THE LAST TIME YOU HAD PROFESSIONAL HELP WITH MAKE UP? MOST DEPARTMENT STORES OFFER OPPORTUNITIES TO UPDATE YOUR LOOK, AND YOU NEED NOT BUY ANYTHING. OR SURF THE WEB AND SEARCH OUT MAKE UP (AND HAIRSTYLES) THAT ARE TRENDY AND FUN. THERE ARE PLENTY OF BUDGET WISE COSMETICS AT THE DRUG STORE SO THAT YOU CAN MASTER A YOUTHFUL LOOK.

 *BRIGHTEN YOUR SMILE. YOU CAN TALK WITH YOUR DENTIST ABOUT TEETH BRIGHTENING OPTIONS OR USE THE HOME VARIETIES. YOU CAN ALSO WEAR A BRIGHT RED LIPSTICK, AS LONG AS YOUR OTHER MAKE UP SUPPORTS THE COLOR. RED LIPSTICK MAKES YOUR TEETH INSTANTLY LOOK WHITER.

 *GET A YOUTHFUL SMILE. YOUNG PEOPLE LAUGH AND SMILE A LOT, YET AS WE AGE, SOMETIMES THE DAILY GRIND GRINDS US RIGHT DOWN. READ A FUNNY BOOK, READ JOKES ON THE INTERNET OR WATCH A MOVIE THAT MAKES YOU LAUGH. PRACTICE YOUR SMILE IN THE MIRROR AND AS YOU GO THROUGH THE DAY, KEEP WEARING IT.

 *EXERCISE. MAKE FITNESS PART OF YOUR EVERY DAY TO STAY YOUTHFUL AND REDUCE EXCESS BODY FAT. YOU DON'T HAVE TO RUN, JOG OR LIFT WEIGHTS, BUT YOU DO NEED TO FIND A PLAN THAT'S FUN.
IF YOU WORK ALONE OR AT HOME, A FITNESS CLASS AT THE GYM WILL CONNECT YOU WITH OTHERS. IF YOU'RE

BUSY AND SURROUNDED BY PEOPLE ALL DAY LONG, A SOLITARY WALK, SWIM OR CYCLE MIGHT BALANCE YOUR LIFE.

*EAT BETTER THAN A YOUTHFUL PERSON. YES, TEENAGERS AND YOUNG ADULTS EAT TOO MUCH FAT, TOO MANY CALORIES AND THINK THAT THEIR BODIES CAN HANDLE IT. AS WE MATURE, WE REALIZE THAT'S NOT TRUE. FOR THIS DAY, AT LEAST, SELECT FOODS THAT SUPPORT YOUR YOUNG LIFESTYLE, SUCH AS FRESH FRUITS, DELICIOUS VEGETABLES AND LOW-FAT PROTEIN.

*TAKE CHANCES. EXPERIMENT TRYING NEW FOODS, NEW MOVIES AND BOOKS, OR STARTING NEW HOBBIES. MINGLE WITH GROUPS YOU MAY NOT KNOW WELL. VOLUNTEER IN YOUR COMMUNITY, ESPECIALLY IN PLACES WHERE THERE WILL BE LOTS OF YOUNG PEOPLE. YOU'LL HAVE A GRANDSTAND VIEW OF WHAT YOUTH DOES, SAYS AND WEARS, AND YOU'LL PICK UP TIPS YOU MIGHT WANT TO USE.

*WATCH WHAT YOU SAY. BANISH TERMS LIKE, "SENIOR MOMENT," AND PHRASES LIKE, "I'M GETTING OLD" FROM YOUR SPEECH. REPLACE THEM WITH, "SOUNDS LIKE FUN" AND "I LIKE NEW THINGS." YOU CAN LOOK SIX YEARS YOUNGER BY TONIGHT WITH THESE TIPS, AND BEST YET, YOU CAN REPEAT THEM TOMORROW AS YOU STAY FIT FOR LIFE.

ABOUT OAKS THE OAKS AT OJAI
The Oaks at Ojai is an affordable fitness destination spa that includes overnight accommodations, three delicious and low-calorie meals a day, choice of 16 fitness classes per day and evening entertainment and seminars. The Oaks offers 46 guest rooms, including private rooms and suites, double lodge rooms and double cottage rooms.

Fitness & Health for the Busy Professional

A charming 1920s hotel-turned-spa in the peaceful town of Ojai, The Oaks offers a variety of activities that allows guests to choose how to work out and take off excess pounds. Activities range from hiking, power walks and in-line skating, belly dancing, hula hoping, yoga, qi gong, water aerobics and other work out classes. A full menu of relaxing and therapeutic spa services is available as well as private consultations with a variety of health experts. The Oaks at Ojai is located at 122 East Ojai Avenue (Ojai's main street).

For more information, visit The Oaks at Ojai online at www.oaksspa.com or call (800) 753-OAKS (6257).
HEALTHY REGARDS,
 ELIZABETH HORTON
GUEST RELATIONS DIRECTOR THE OAKS AT OJAI
FIND US ON FACEBOOK! ~ TWITTER ~ ACORN
NEWSLETTER 122 EAST OJAI AVENUE OJAI, CA 93023
805.646.5573 X 150
GO GREEN, KEEP IT ON THE SCREEN!

Websites of Interest

Visit the American Council on Exercise web site – www.acefitness.com or call their toll free number, 1-800-825-3636. They provide resources for fitness products and services and a list of certified trainers.

Also visit: http://does.ors.od.nih.gov/fitness/. They serve the NIH community (National Institutes of Health) and offer classes on yoga, yoga and aerobics.

When having children, getting up before they do to get your workout in is ideal. Not only are you improving your health and fitness level, you are also having your own time "alone" time, which mothers rarely have anymore.

Get 30min of something in (walk, walk/jog, video, lifting, etc)

Try new exercises: classes, martial arts, belly dancing, etc - there are so many options, the more you like it, the more you will go

Stop putting yourself last! Make time for you, don't you deserve it!?

Lift weights, you will see more change in your body by lifting weights than anything else.

If walking your dog, do walking lunges, side shuffles, high knees, walk backwards, etc, mix it up.

Do push-ups every morning when you get up - everyone has time for them. You will work your core, chest, back, shoulders and arms. You will get stronger in a short time frame.

Diets are terrible, they are not sustainable, if you lose weight on them most gain it all back, if not more, it needs to be a lifestyle, something you can do forever. 1) eating breakfast is huge 2)always have protein at every meal 3)always have a carb at every meal (fruit or veggies are carbs) and 4) eat good fats - coconut oil, butter and olive oil, you need good fats to burn fat and to fill you up
Get rid of all the fat free junk, it isn't real food. Eat real food.

No fast food, nothing from a box, no sodas, little to no alcohol - that's the big one and the hardest one for most

80/20 rule - 80% of the time eat healthy
Eat to give yourself energy

Hope this helps you!

Health and Abundance,

Alison

Ali McWilliams Personal Fitness, LLC

"Life is too short for drama & petty things, so kiss slowly, laugh insanely, love truly and forgive quickly."-Unknown

Become a FACEBOOK FAN
http://www.facebook.com/alimcwilliamspf
Check out the WEBSITE
http://www.alimcwilliams.com/
Learn more at my BLOG
http://www.alimcwilliams.com/blog/
Follow me on TWITTER:
http://twitter.com/alimcwilliamspf

Lastly, drop by the Mayo Clinic web site: www.mayoclinic.com. Scroll down the page and under the sub-heading "Live Well", click on "fitness."

Conclusion

When you started reading this book, chances are you felt that you could *never* incorporate a fitness program into your busy lifestyle. Now, however, the chances are quite good that you're confident, enthusiastic, and ready to start becoming fit!

Remember, please, some of the cardinal rules that we've covered here. Though we won't recap them all – because you can re-read any section of the book that you wish! – Let's just highlight a few of the most important principles that you should bear in mind as you move forward:

- ☑ don't do too much at once; start slow, and build a foundation of fitness

- ☑ Exercise for *more* than cosmetic appeal; your inner-body needs to be fit, too (especially as you age!)

- ☑ plan ahead and stay in hotels that offer you fitness equipment

☑ carry essential fitness tools with you as you travel

☑ Eat healthy and properly so that you don't "hit the wall" as you become fit!

☑ Keep a record of your successes (through a journal or log)

☑ Exercise with friends or other people who share a common fitness interest with you (and make NEW friends in the process!)

☑ Manage your time effectively so that you can incorporate a fitness program – large or small – into your daily routine.

Now that you've obtained the information you need, the next step is up to you. Consult the resources recommended in this book, including the websites, and build an exercise program into your life.

What will your rewards be for your efforts? Statistically, you'll:

- ➢ look better
- ➢ feel better
- ➢ have a higher quality of life

And, in case it matters to you..

- ➢ You'll be the ENVY of all of your busy friends and relatives who want to know how someone as busy as YOU has become so FIT!

The SECRET

- of Weight Loss

1 pound of fat = 3500 Calories

If you burn 5500 calories a day and only take in 2000, you could lose a pound a day.

The average sedentary day you burn about 2500 calories just sleeping and sitting on your butt.
(This was my average day for work)

You really don't want to lose more than 5 pounds a week though.

The recommended minimum intake to remain healthy is 1200/day for females and 1500/day for males.

I would encourage you to track or journal your food intake during this program. If you are really overweight I would encourage you to reduce caloric intake first, this will help reduce the pressure on your joints during exercise. Consult a physician prior to beginning an exercise program.

A free resource that helped me when I got started is www.CALORIECOUNT.com.

You can track what you eat and see your goals, it also shows the calorie count of many foods.

It will give you an initial assessment, Example, for me because of my height and starting weight the site recommended that I try to take in a minimum of 2100 calories a day.

If you can burn more calories in a day than you intake it will start to melt off.

Imagine how many more calories and how much faster you will lose the fat if you add exercise?

Count on it!

Another resource I used when I traveled was a pocket guide from www.THECALORIEKING.com

This amazing guide has all kinds of calorie numbers for all kinds of foods and most of the dining out restaurants you may frequent.

There even apps available for your personal cell phone or other personal device that you can use to look up calories or keep track of your diet.

The other secret to keeping up with your fitness is to add a good quality multivitamin/mineral supplement.

I still believe that the best vitamin/mineral supplement I have ever taken was DoubleX from Amway. If you know a distributor, invest in yourself, if you are a distributor, you should definitely be taking advantage of your discount pricing.

I have tried hundreds of supplements and this one was the most effective in changing my health and energy levels.

To find a local distributor of DoubleX you can go to www.amway.com. It is worth every penny of the investment!

If you are in a network marketing program with supplements you definitely want to take advantage of your discount, there are so many great products out there from many great companies and organizations.

The great thing about being in an **MLM** business that has nutritional products is that to an extent some of those products may be tax deductable.

Again. If you have access to those products, take advantage of it!

The only way you will start to lose weight and stay fit is to take action.

The number one way to gain weight and lose your health is to just sit on your rear and keep stuffing your face.

Start out small. Start walking around the block, walking up the stairs, parking farther away, eating less, boxing up half of your meal in a restaurant as soon as you get it, all of these small things will help. Before you know it you will enjoy working out, make better food choices and start feeling more energy.

Additional resources and products for busy people!

"Movement Snacks"
While they won't keep you totally fit, they will renew energy and help you get out of the sedentary position that we are all facing in our world today.
Product link:
http://www.exuberantanimal.com/library/movement_snacks/index.html

www.tao-well.com

A take-anywhere, do-any-time, total-body-workout to stay fit.

RESVERATROL   Winner of:

Best of Natural Beauty Award by Better Nutrition Magazine
Best New Supplements of the Year by Vitamin Retailer Magazine
Best of Supplements Award by Better Nutrition Magazine

Resveratrol is the element found in red wine grapes that hold various health benefits. There was recent study that was just released regarding its ability to maximize caloric burn during workouts, which could be an interesting addition for your feature. Also, it has been clinically proven to increase energy to help individuals workout longer and harder.

www.Reserveage.com

My name is Alison Pollock.. In the last two years, I have lost 70 pounds and kept it off. I have also gone from being completely sedentary to completing 3 half marathons and one triathlon. I attribute my success to my Health Coach, Peter K, and his fitness kit called "5 Minutes To Fitness +". Peter's kit comes complete with one set of resistance bands, an instructional DVD, and a nutrition book. The instructional DVD takes you through a total body workout that is completed in just 5 minutes.

Peter K MS, PT is a world renowned speaker, author, and a leading authority on health and fitness .

Thank you!
Allison
Associate, Peter K Fitness
www.peterkfitness.com

Hello!
I know a lot about helping people "fit fitness" into their lives. As a former Navy SEAL and current father of four sons under 8 years old, it's become my life's work and passion to figure out how to stay fit despite the many challenges of daily life.

I started a company that creates custom decks of playing cards with exercises on them. The idea is to have a simple, convenient, and fun way to "deal yourself a workout" anytime, anywhere. Each card takes about 1 minute to complete, so a 5-minute workout would call for the user to select 5 cards from the deck. This is an ideal way to integrate small bouts of fitness into your life because it is easy to start and stop - and initimidating.

Since we started with "FitDeck Bodyweight" (our flagship

title) several years ago, we've expanded to 34 different titles ranging from FitDeck Office, to Stretch, to Prenatal, to Navy SEAL. These "EXERCISE PLAYING CARDS" are unique, fun, and AFFORDABLE ($9.95 - $16.95).

Now that we have expanded to 34 new and different titles, there is not one person who cannot find a FitDeck that suits their needs - men, women, kids, grandparents.

FitDeck is a unique deck of playing cards that contains exercises instead of the normal playing card faces.
The exercises have three different fitness levels to accommodate players of all ages and abilities.

www.fitdeck.com

Here's a sampling of our library of titles:

FitDeck Bodyweight - MEN
FitDeck Junior - kids
FitDeck Senior
FitDeck Prenatal - mom
FitDeck Postnatal - mom
FitDeck Yoga
FitDeck Pilates - moms and dads
FitDeck Stretch
FitDeck Navy SEAL - MEN
FitDeck Office
FitDeck Playground
FitDeck Baby Stroller - mom and men
FitDeck Travel
FitDeck Combat Sports
FitDeck Firefighter
FitDeck Stairs
FitDeck Exercise Ball
FitDeck Balance Dome
FitDeck Dumbbell
FitDeck Resistance Tube

Fitness & Health for the Busy Professional

FitDeck Pull Up Bar
FitDeck Kettlebell
FitDeck Toning Ball
FitDeck Exercise Bar

Phil Black
FitDeck, Inc.
San Diego, CA 92122
800-226-6022
www.fitdeck.com
On Twitter: http://www.twitter.com/FitDeck
On Facebook: http://www.facebook.com/FitDeck

Dr. Marc Tinsley is a health, fitness, and wellness expert who works with organizations who want to stop losing money and be more productive by taking better care of themselves and their members. He takes the fear, difficulty, mystery, and confusion out of health, wellness, and fitness with keynotes, breakouts, workshops, in-services, teleseminars, webinars, coaching, and consulting.

He is the founder of Fitness For The Rest of Us(tm).

Wellness: Your Competitive Advantage

Is Your Job Making You Fat? * Be Active, Be Healthy * Reforming Your Health

Taking Care of Yourself When You're Taking Care of Business

Motivation, Inspiration, Perspiration, and Education

Fit, Unfit, or Misfit?

Fitness & Health for the Busy Professional

Become a fan at http://facebook.DrMarcTinsley.com

http://LinkedIn.DrMarcTinsley.com

http://twitter.DrMarcTinsley.com

http://Wellsphere.DrMarcTinsley.com

http://bizjournals.DrMarcTinsley.com

DrTinsley@TinsleyHealth.com

www.DrMarcTinsley.com

NATURAL EYE CARE

We are among the leading experts on nutrition and vision. One of the areas that keeps us busy is computer eye strain, and helping professionals maintain healthy vision who use computers all day.

Take care,

Michael Edson, MS, L.Ac.
www.naturaleyecare.com

Don't forget to request our free monthly newsletter on natural eye care and holistic health at our website above.

Greetings!

I wanted to let you know that I've been working with leading nutrition, fitness and online weight-loss program, EDIETS.COM! They have been an industry leader for over a decade and have created numerous easy and effective ways for losing weight and KEEPING it off. Many busy professionals may be overwhelmed with taking care of themselves with their current workload as it is, so why add to the stress of it by worrying about those extra pounds?

eDiets has great online diet plans, meal delivery plans, and even an at-home Boot Camp program to do on your time off that are affordable and effective for getting rid of the extra weight without the fuss! The best thing about the eDiets plans is that they are extremely nutritious and balanced, meaning you get all the essential vitamins and minerals needed. Below are some tips from the eDiets experts on how busy professionals can still control their weight, despite their hectic schedule.

DON'T STARVE YOURSELF – EAT HEALTHY To lose weight and keep it off eat smaller portions more frequently.

A healthy diet should be low in saturated fat and be full of fruits, vegetables and lean proteins. Here are 2 easy and affordable ways to get support for your healthier eating habits:

1) EDIETS ONLINE DIET PLAN: Day by day meal plan ideas sent to you online that will fit your lifestyle. With 24/7 access and personalized diet and fitness advice from experts, a plan can be designed to fit YOUR lifestyle. eDiets plans incorporate your favorite foods, so you don't have to feel like you are sacrificing any aspect of your life. These plans teach you about nutritional value of food, which is priceless for long-term results.

* For a limited time, new subscribers can receive 1 full week FREE to try it out with the exclusive promo code: FREEWK. Full details available here: www.eDiets.com/deals

2) MEAL DELIVERY PLANS: Don't have time to cook or shop for healthy food? No problem. The website offers a great service that will change your habits of eating junk food to those that will help you lose weight and increase wellness. The wide variety of nutritious meal plans (perfect if you are breast-feeding to maintain all the healthy vitamins and minerals for your baby) that eDiets offers range from Mediterranean to glycemic impact foods, so there is a plan for every one!

* You can focus on cooking for your baby, and save time on cooking for yourself.
* For a limited time, you can sign up now and get a FREE FIRST WEEK of meals. Full details available here: www.eDiets.com/deals

GET REGULAR EXERCISE
You are probably already running around with your boss buzzing in your ear, but if you ever get a minute of solitude, consider using that time to do some simple exercises like squats, push-ups, sit-ups, lunges, and jumping jacks. Building muscle helps burn fat and it's likely that your muscles began to weaken from all your desk side hours- take some time to get them strong once again! Besides with a little midday exercise you'll get a burst of energy without the extra caffeine! Need a little work out boost?

3) THE EDIETS BEST BODY BOOT CAMP is once again taking place. Given that you may not be able to leave the house much, Boot Camp is the perfect solution to getting a workout routine.

Boot camp exercises are designed to burn fat right where you need to! Unlike with other programs, the eDiets trainer checks in with you regularly to support you and monitor progress for a slimmer you in just 6 weeks!

Getting into shape and dieting aren't the easiest or the most fun things to do, but with the help of eDiets, anyone can lose up to 10 lbs in just 5 weeks to ensure the best body possible. If the program does not work, eDiets will give another 6 months on the house!

ABOUT EDIETS.COM: eDiets.com, Inc. is a leading provider of personalized nutrition, fitness and weight-loss programs. eDiets features its award-winning, fresh-prepared diet meal delivery service as one of the more than 20 popular diet plans on its flagship site, www.eDiets.com. The company also provides a broad range of customized wellness and weight management solutions for Fortune 500 clients. Active eDiets members achieve generally expected weight loss of 10 pounds during the first 5 weeks of an eDiets program._

Looking forward to your Healthy Choices!

Marissa Harrell

WWW.NATREN.COM

We have many customers who take our Natren Healthy Trinity Probiotic Pill once a day to help support their immunity and help ensure their health and well-being. For more information, please see attached.

Thank you!
ADRIANA TRENEV PLUT

WWW.TRUTHABOUTPROBIOTICS.COM

www.physiic.com

Exercise is an important part of my daily routine despite my busy schedule. I need workouts that are exciting and effective, so I choose group exercise classes. Unfortunately, group exercise usually means extra time spent commuting to the studio or gym, assuming I can even find a yoga, or strength training class that fits my schedule.
Luckily, I have access to interactive fitness classes on physiic.com that I can take from home. An interactive fitness class is a live, group exercise class that is accessible online. I get personalized, interactive fitness instruction by videoconference from a wide selection of talented health and wellness professionals who post live classes daily.

Sincerely,

Justin Tuttle
www.physiic.com

www.E-mealz.com

Hi Troy,

Everyday men and women come home and face the arduous task of figuring out the answer to the dinner dilemma. "What will I make for dinner tonight?" It makes it really easy after a long day, to just give in to the temptation to run through the drive through if you don't already have a plan in place for losing weight and what to do for dinner. That's where E-mealz comes in. E-Mealz relies on a team of experienced meal planners, writers and editors to create new menus every week that are designed around grocery store sales, seasonal specials and diet preferences. Diet preferences include Weight Watchers, low fat, and vegetarian to name a few. For $5.00 per month, subscribers download a recipe plan online for the week with a matching aisle-by-aisle grocery list. The easy-to-follow recipes usually contain fewer than seven ingredients to allow for prep times of less than 30 minutes. We have been spoken of highly already in this regard in the Redbook February 2010 issue. One Red Book reader slimmed down from a size 20 to a size 10 with the help of E-mealz!

Thank you,
Heather Brown
Product Development & Marketing E-mealz Inc

FuelBelt

FuelBelt gear essential for the active lifestyle FuelBelt gear is a must have for the busy individual who is trying to stay healthy. Hydrating on runs is extremely important for getting the most out of your works and staying safe. Fill up your bottles and go for a hands free run.
Check out our product line at www.fuelbelt.com

fuelbelt.com | xtri.com | 2010 FuelBelt Catalog

Follow us on Twitter @FuelBelt

Yumnuts Naturals.

 Yumnuts are all-natural, dry-roasted and flavored cashews that are available in six flavors, (Cajun, Chili Lime, Chocolate, Honey, Sea Salt and Toasted Coconut) all of which are free of anything artificial, gluten and trans fats. We believe our nuts are nature's perfect snack because they provide the protein, smart fats and minerals to fuel a healthy lifestyle.

In order to address our health-conscious target audience, we have been sampling Yumnuts at triathlons, bicycle races, heath clubs and soccer tournaments. The positive response has been fantastic and we have grown rapidly since we started in March 2009. Since then, we have been picked up by Whole Foods, Stop & Shop, Kroger and Roche Brothers to name a few, as well as several independent markets.

In addition to snacking on our cashews, many loyal fans have used our Yumnuts as a tasty and healthy addition to recipes and snacks. Here are a few examples of how Yumnuts can be added to traditional favorites:

Cajun Yumnuts to top your favorite stir-fry

Chocolate Yumnuts baked into banana bread

Honey Yumnuts over yogurt

Toasted Coconut Yumnuts to crust tilapia.

Life is short, remember to say Yum!

Yumnuts Naturals
65 East Avenue | 3rd Floor
Norwalk, CT | 06851
www.yumnutsnaturals.com

Chicago-based Celebrity Fitness Trainer (and my personal body transformation guru) John Hall would be a great resource for you. I'm a witness that he can show busy professionals like me how to use little or no equipment and still stay in shape. I'm a mom, TV/Radio Personality and entrepreneur here in Chicago. My time is extremely limited. However, Thanks to John I know how to get a workout in even if I only have 15 minutes to spare in between taping shows or waiting at the airport. Over the past year I have lost 30 lbs! You can see my transformation here: www.moniquecaradine.com/transformation   Anyway, I've learned how to use my own body weight to workout thanks to John. If you want to talk to him let me know or reach him directly at john@johnhallstudios.com

Thanks and good luck with your project! Monique Caradine
TV/Radio Personality
President
Momentum Media Group, Inc.
Executive Media Coaching for Women Entrepreneurs

www.MoniqueCaradine.com

www.breakpal.com

A lot of people use Break Pal. Break Palt fits micro-workouts into the day.
3-4 minute exercises every 30-60 minutes add up to a full workout at the end of the day and boosts productivity too.

http://www.breakpal.com

Phil Weaver

I'm a Chiropractor in California, and write a health blog. I recently wrote a post that may be right up your ally.

It talks about not only having to schedule your workout time, but all of the accessory activities that go along with it, and having to have a system to integrate these tasks into your daily routine. Feel free to visit:

http://www.sactownhealth.com/2010/08/health-success-your-dialy-routine/

Dr. Derek Gibbons, D.C.

TROY'S REVIEW: Stand Up Paddling or SUP is one of the hottest new fitness activities. It has been featured in many leading magazines. If you live near water, you will want to check it out!!!

When I'm busy, and believe me I'm busy (I own and operate a stand up paddle board shop with my husband and also teach Pilates), I choose workouts that give me the most benefits for the time involved. Stand up paddling (SUP) covers all the bases in terms of fitness. It's a toes to nose workout. The muscles of the feet are strengthened (many people report higher, stronger arches), the calves, thighs and glutes are toned. Just balancing on the board requires an engaged core at all times. Proper paddle technique generates power from the arms, upper back and, most of all, the obliques. Calories can be burned faster than with an activity like running because each paddle stroke has both strengthening and cardiovascular benefits. Plus, there are the mind-body benefits. The sensation of walking on water is often referred to by SUPers as "aqua-therapy". Not to mention the fact that that you're outside enjoying nature. I've been a fitness enthusiast my entiere life and SUP is truly the most comprehensive form of exercise I've come across yet it doesn't feel like working out because it's so much fun! Lainey Booth, co-owner of Stand Up Paddle Flatwater & Stand Up Paddle Bend. Stand Up Paddle Flatwater is a family-owned online retailer that offers everything necessary to stand up paddle, including SUP boards, paddles, accessories, apparel, rentals, and information. A flagship store, Stand Up Paddle Bend, is located at 550 SW Industrial Way, #115, Bend, Oregon 97702. Lainey@StandUpPaddleFlatwater.com

Stand Up Paddle Flatwater Facebook

Twitter

Blog

ExerciseFriends.com is the country's largest health and exercise site for people who find it better to get healthy through activities with other people. we have all kinds of stories about busy people who found other busy people with the same schedule, same goals, same level of skill to do healthy things together.

There is a new dynamic in the exercise world, and it is all about accountability---having a partner to do it with gets it done.
Jay Valentine

www.exercisefriends.com

Hi Troy,

My name is Stephanie, and I'm a fun Health & Fitness Expert. I do TV segments and train private clients on how to incorporate fitness into their everyday lives. I created the Cubicle Crunch: http://www.stepitupwithsteph.com/tag/cubicle_crunch/ and other things to do around the house, at work, and after work to make time for even a 5 minute run, 50 crunches, and other things to do for your body.

I believe that all of this comes with a shift in your MINDSET - being active doesn't need to involve an hour at the gym. Being active and fit is a mindset and once working out is not viewed as a burden or a chore, it is seen as something fun to do and a happy part of a busy day.

Thanks,Stephanie

--

To the life that YOU want,
Stephanie Mansour, CEO Step It Up with Steph
Health & Fitness Expert
Body Image & Confidence Coach

Quick, free workouts: Turbo Abs, Butts, Yoga, & more!
www.StepItUpwithSteph.com

Troy's Note: Steph is full of energy and very innovative, she really makes fitness an easy part of any moment in your day. Check out her videos and programs!!

Troy A. Bonar
"The Safety Samurai"™
Speaker, Author, and Consultant

Troy A. Bonar nicknamed "The Safety Samurai"™ is a leading authority on safety, leadership, and mentoring. Troy has over 20 years of business experience and 20+ years of martial arts study. He combines his life experiences with ancient wisdom to assist business and individuals in achieving success in today's ever changing society. Troy is a member of the National Speakers Association, the International Speakers Network. He currently holds master trainer certification and was recently named one of the 'Top 5 Trainers in the World'. Troy's books, seminars, and keynote speeches are interactive, engaging, humorous, and 'life challenging'.

Troy A. Bonar
President
Safety Personnel Services, Inc.
P.O. Box 6333
Abilene, TX 79608
Email:TroyBonar@live.com

More about
Troy A. Bonar MST

Originally from Charlevoix Michigan, Troy grew up in the countryside and enjoyed the 4 seasons that Northern Michigan had to offer. He was an active member of community organizations, participated in many school programs and also spent time playing team sports including, football, basketball, soccer and the summer youth bowling league. Troy was also a member of the International Club, and Future Problem Solvers of America.

Little Known Fact

Troy has had frostbite and hypothermia more than once.
(Now he lives in the South)

Troy began working at the age of 10. He started as most kids do, mowing lawns, and doing odd jobs, one of which was to collect eggs at a local poultry farm. Troy then moved on to working various positions throughout his life including working at a golf course, working at a retail clothing store, working in a high end jewelry store, construction, brick laying, roofing, vehicle detail, first mate on a yacht, professional driver, program relocation specialist, general maintenance, landscaper, youth outreach coordinator, martial arts instructor, fossil recovery diver, bartender, waiter, bouncer, short order cook, farm hand, exhibit hall/ convention support staff, newspaper media room technician, safety instructor, intelligence specialist, bodyguard, security consultant, author, speaker, expert witness, aerobics instructor, personal trainer, film producer, food critic, lifeguard, actor, religious advisor, cinematographer, mountain guide, wholesale distributer, natural therapy consultant, acupuncturist, product tester, film critic, event planner, and is working on his next experience that will help him expand his knowledge. Troy believes that there is always work if you look for it, and to treat every job as an opportunity for self improvement. Troy has been known to work 3 jobs at a time when needed to generate capital for business and investment opportunities.

Little Known Fact:

Troy reads or listens to at least 2 business, finance, and improvement books per week.

 When Troy was 14 he began working for local business owners to earn money to be a Student Ambassador to the USSR or former Soviet Union. During this time Troy began working for a local entrepreneur who became a huge influence in his life, for the next 3 years he would meet with local business owners to have coffee in the mornings and learn business strategies and concerns. This mentorship had a great influence on Troy's business insight and understanding. Troy not only worked for this great business minded person, but he also started his own landscaping business which was very rewarding but seasonal in Northern Michigan.

Little known fact:

Troy A. Bonar was the first Official Student Mascot for the Charlevoix Rayders he served as the Mascot for 2.5 years.

Troy graduated as the President of his class and decided that he would serve his country in the U.S. Air Force.

During his time of service Troy was honored to be a part of many special assignments and deployments.

Little known fact:

Troy also served as a Bugler for the USAF Honor Guard and performed over 700 honors.

Flash Back: Troy began studying martial arts when he was 12 years old and formally joined the World Kuk Sool Won Association at the age of 17.

Troy was also a student of Shotokan Karate, Tang Soo do, Hapkido, Aikido, and Iado. Troy traveled extensively and was an instructor in Abilene TX for over 10 years.

In 1996 Troy started a direct distribution company Bonar & Associates International.

When Troy got out of the Air Force he took a 3 year position with a business consulting and training company in Abilene, TX.

In 2000 Troy started Safety Personnel Services, Inc. This originally began as a personnel provider for project safety. The company began to grow as clients requested further services. The business has continued to evolve to meet industry demands, including not only Safety, but Human Resource Management, Security, and Executive Protection resources and training.

Little known Fact:

Troy has traveled to 43 of the 50 United States and is going to visit them all!

In the summer of 1997 Troy was involved in a civil incident where an explosion killed the man next to him and injured 17 others. Troy responded to the incident and facilitated first aid care for multiple victims until responders could arrive.

This incident made him realize that people needed to be trained on proper response. Many people were willing to help but had no idea of what needed to be done and many were misinformed and could have caused further harm do to outdated information and instruction.

This incident was the start of Troy's passion to educated and inspire others to be ready to respond in the event of an incident and to become better prepared in every aspect of their life.

Troy began his journey as a speaker by volunteering for the American Red Cross to help teach readiness courses. He eventually was put on staff as an instructor for approximately 2 years.

Little known Fact

Troy is a world champion knife thrower.

Troy was offered a safety and training position with a local contractor and stopped teaching martial arts as a full time profession (now he only teaches seminar and private lessons).

Troy was still committed to the mission of the American Red Cross and was invited to serve as an advisory board member and did so for 2 years until the restructuring of the American Red Cross.

Troy began to see the need for fresh ideas and participation from passionate leading authorities on topics of interest in the business world. In 2008 Troy began the journey to become a professional speaker to help industries motivate and educate their people.

Troy's passion is to keep it real and also to help employees, supervisors, and business owners take their profession to the next level.

Little Known Fact:

Troy has watched over 10,267 films/productions in his lifetime, and he prefers not to watch the same film twice.

Complacency and mediocrity have crept into many areas of business and his programs help to create a desire for excellence and constant improvement in all areas of our daily life.

Troy's wealth of knowledge and experience in the business industry combined with over 20 years of martial arts philosophy have helped him connect with all different types of people.

Troy believes family, friends, and coworkers are all interconnected and our actions can seriously affect others. He speaks about personal responsibility and the positive changes that can happen when we start to account for who we are, what we do, and how we do it.

Little Known Fact

Troy was the youngest of 80+ grand children for 12 years

Troy takes driving seriously; he usually travels over 60,000 miles a year on the road. He has survived 8 vehicle totaling collisions and numerous smaller incidents on the road. Troy believes there is no such thing as an accident and encourages everyone to watch out for each other.

If you want someone who keeps it real, is down to earth, relates easily with your people, humorous, and easy to work with, hire Troy Bonar to come and speak to your group.

Fitness & Health for the Busy Professional

Troy's Books and Resources

GPS for Success: Goals and Proven Strategies for Success with Co Authors Stephen Covey, Les Brown and Dr. John Gray

OSHA SURVIVAL: Program 1 Inspections

OSHA SURVIVAL: Program 2 Training

OSHA SURVIVAL: Program 3 Regulations

Employee to Professional: How to Get More Time, Money, and Respect from Your Job.

Safety Success: 7 Simple Steps for Employees

Safety Success: 7 Simple Steps for Supervision

Safety Success 7 Simple Steps for Owners and Management

Samurai Success: Ancient Principles for Today's Working Warrior.

Bushido Business: The Fine Art of the Business Professional with Co Authors Brian Tracey, Tom Hopkins, and Stephen Covey

Fitness & Health for the Busy Professional

Driving Safety: The Road Warriors Survival Guide

Airport Survival: Tips from Diehard Travelers.

365 Safety Tips

365 Safety Tips: Work

365 Safety Tips: Home

365 Safety Tips: Recreation

365 Safety Tips: Travel/Vacation

Mastering the Art of Success with Co Authors Jack Canfield, Mark Victor Hansen, and Les Brown

Safety Leadership

Safety Influence

The Safety Leader

SafetyMasterminds.com
A great program for professionals and leaders is the

This program not only allows networking between members, but members are given access to top industry professionals. These monthly seminars and resources worth thousands of dollars are given to subscribing members . SafetyMasterminds.com gives access to industry experts and leading authorities and is one of best keys to continuous improvement of your safety programs.
Visit www.safetymasterminds.com for further information on becoming a part of this elite membership program that will give you access to the best to be the best.

Safety Success Bootcamps:

Troy's innovative 2 & 3 Day workshops to get your safety program on the track to the success your company deserves.

This is not about regulations; this is the backbone to great safety, the secrets, the tips, the resources and the best practices of proven success.

"Connection is Key!"
-Jonathan Sprinkles

Find Troy on Facebook Fan Pages
- "The Samurai of Success" motivation and tips for daily success in your life.

-"The Safety Samurai" Safety information resources and tips.

Connect with Troy Bonar on LinkedIn

Find Troy Bonar on Twitter too!

Fitness & Health for the Busy Professional

Awards and Recognition Program

Troy Bonar serves as the President of Professionals of the World ™ an international registry of professionals, trades persons, and business owners.

Professionals of the World ™ is a 3rd party recognition program which can be used to recognize your business, personnel or professionals for their achievements.

Visit www.professionalsoftheworld.com Or contact troybonar@live.com for the current information.

Awards include:
Incident / injury Free Awards
Driving Safety
Safety Awards (continued on next page)
Leadership
Team
Employee
Top 10
Innovation
#1 in (your industry)
Best of (year)
Diversity
Innovative Program
….and more.

Visit www.professionalsoftheworld.com for more details on awards and recognition.

Enjoyed it? Pass it on to a friend, family member or co-worker.

Reader Log

"I have read this book and I am passing it on to you!"

1_____

2_____

3_____

4_____

5_____

6_____

7_____

8_____

9_____

10_____

11_____

12_____

13_____

14_____

15_____

www.ingramcontent.com/pod-product-compliance
Lightning Source LLC
Chambersburg PA
CBHW060250290526
45789CB00001B/279